Praise for
Visions, Trips, and Crowded Rooms

"David Kessler writes of a world that is rarely talked about, much less examined with such sensitivity. His stories reveal dimensions of the death experience that are anything but depressing, and at times absolutely joyful. In a book filled with intriguing and inspirational tales, Kessler makes a compelling argument that death is not the end."

— **Marianne Williamson**, the *New York Times* best-selling author of *The Age of Miracles* and *A Course in Weight Loss*

"I so remember David Kessler in the old days of *The Hayride*, a support group I started in West Hollywood. He and his work were so vital and so heartwarming to our group, who shared those frightening moments of crises in the early days of the AIDS epidemic. His very presence with those approaching death was like being enveloped in a safe, cozy space. No harm could come to you if David was around. In fact, I recently asked him to be there when it is my time to go. This book shares David's wisdom and his love, and helps all of us who enter unknown waters."

— **Louise Hay**, the *New York Times* best-selling author of *You Can Heal Your Life*

VISIONS, TRIPS, AND CROWDED ROOMS

ALSO BY DAVID KESSLER

*ON GRIEF AND GRIEVING: Finding the Meaning of Grief
Through the Five Stages of Loss*
(co-authored with Elisabeth Kübler-Ross)

*LIFE LESSONS: Two Experts on Death and Dying Teach
Us About the Mysteries of Life and Living*
(co-authored with Elisabeth Kübler-Ross)

*THE NEEDS OF THE DYING: A Guide for Bringing Hope,
Comfort, and Love to Life's Final Chapter*

*YOU CAN HEAL YOUR HEART: Finding Peace After a
Breakup, Divorce, or Death*
(co-authored with Louise Hay)

VISIONS, TRIPS, AND CROWDED ROOMS

Who and What You See
Before You Die

David Kessler

HAY HOUSE, INC.
Carlsbad, California • New York City
London • Sydney • New Delhi

Published in the United States by: Hay House, Inc.: www.hayhouse.com • *Published in Australia by:* Hay House Australia Pty. Ltd.: www.hayhouse.com.au • *Published in the United Kingdom by:* Hay House UK, Ltd.: www.hayhouse.co.uk • *Published in India by:* Hay House Publishers India: www.hayhouse.co.in

Editorial supervision: Jill Kramer • *Project editor:* Lisa Mitchell
Design: Nick C. Welch

Library of Congress Cataloging-in-Publication Data

Kessler, David.
 Visions, trips, and crowded rooms : who and what you see before you die / David Kessler.
  p. cm.
 ISBN 978-1-4019-2542-0 (hbk. : alk. paper) 1. Deathbed hallucinations. 2. Death--Psychological aspects. 3. Terminally ill--Psychology. I. Title.
 BF1063.D4K47 2010
 155.9'37--dc22

2009050707

Tradepaper ISBN: 978-1-4019-2543-7
E-book ISBN: 978-1-4019-2850-6

22 21 20 19 18 17 16 15

1st edition, May 2010
2nd edition, May 2011

SUSTAINABLE FORESTRY INITIATIVE
Certified Chain of Custody
Promoting Sustainable Forestry
www.sfiprogram.org
SFI-01268
SFI label applies to the text stock

Printed in the United States of America

For Richard, David, and India

CONTENTS

CONTENTS

A NOTE TO THE READER

This book is the result of personal experiences of health-care professionals and clergy members, as well as those who have lost loved ones. The contributors have not received any pay or recognition; rather, they have shared their stories in the hope that readers will come away less afraid and with a deeper understanding about what happens in our final moments of life. These firsthand accounts suggest that deathbed visions are normal and actually common, and they were culled from believers and skeptics alike, with no agenda. The stories contained within these pages are very similar, but that is the point. The fact that people from all over the world have seen the same things in their last chapter of life is what makes these experiences remarkable.

This book is simply a report from the front lines, featuring stories of average people, in their own words, experiencing extraordinary events.

(**Editor's note:** All stories have been edited
for length and clarity.)

PREFACE

When people ask me what I do, I pause and cringe a little. Do I tell them that I write books on death and dying? Or do I tell them that I was first trained as a nurse and now I run a highly regarded and unique end-of-life program at the fifth-largest hospital system in Los Angeles? Do I explain that I'm a specialist police reserve officer on the trauma team, as well as being a member of the Red Cross disaster team? Or that I trained for a pilot's license and worked on two aviation disasters?

I know it can be confusing, so I often say that I'm a hybrid of all those things. Unlike my mentor, Elisabeth Kübler-Ross, who mostly worked with death in the hospital setting, I'm trained as a modern-day thanatologist; in other words, I don't only deal with death in the hospital or hospice, but also at crime scenes, plane crashes, and even bioterror attacks. I follow death wherever it calls me. When I look back on my reasons for following this unusual path, I see that my career choices weren't random. It was my destiny to become who I am because of one particular day when I was 12 years old.

My mother battled health problems throughout much of my life. On New Year's Eve 1972, I walked into her bedroom, where she was ailing. I gave her a kiss and said, "Mom, 1973 will be the year you get better." Within days, as she endured severe kidney failure, she was transferred from our local VA hospital to one that was much larger and better equipped.

My father and I sometimes stayed at a hotel across the park from the hospital when we had the money. We mostly sat in the hospital's lobby since my mother was in an intensive care unit, which only allowed visitors every two hours for ten minutes. One morning we were on our way to see Mom when there was sudden activity around our hotel. Everyone outside began running as shots were fired. Evidently, there was a sniper on top of the building. Within seconds, police were everywhere while people rushed into the adjoining buildings for cover. It was actually pretty exciting stuff for a child who had been so bored sitting in the hospital for days on end.

Dad and I eventually made our way over to see Mom and were told that she didn't have long to live. She died alone that day, but that's the way it happened back then. Families (especially children) were often not allowed to be present during a patient's final moments; and when they were, it was at the mercy of the caretakers. My mother's doctor reluctantly agreed to let my father see her, but said that I could not. When the nurse came to take Dad to Mom's room, I went along, hoping I wouldn't get caught.

The nurse led us to the bed where my mother's lifeless body lay; and as difficult as it was, I was actually relieved to be face-to-face with her without all the machines and tubes. I felt little privacy, though, because there were 17 other patients in the ward. The nurse who brought us in also stood close by—never leaving us alone—ready to whisk us out when our brief time allotment was up.

Before the day was over, I took my first plane ride. Since my mother had just died, as a well-meaning gesture, the pilots invited me into the cockpit to "help" them fly the plane. Even though I appreciated the gesture, it was all but lost on me. I clearly remember looking out from the cockpit, feeling utterly overwhelmed, knowing that what I'd seen with my mother wasn't how death was supposed to be.

When I take a look at my career choices—dealing with death in the medical world, becoming a reserve police officer, and learning to fly a plane—I see that they were all attempts to gain back the control I'd lost on the day my mother died. Once I found a healing process for myself, I felt that I'd gained a special insight and could help others. Today, I'm the one who could have helped that young boy who was in so much distress. My career is living proof that we teach what we need to learn.

I recently watched a peer of mine featured on *60 Minutes*. He's a medical doctor and was on the show to discuss the idea that too much technology is used at the end of life. He presented his case so well, in fact, that I would have been hard-pressed to do better. As he spoke, I thought back to the numerous families I've worked with in the ICU who kept their loved ones alive with artificial equipment in a futile attempt to restore their health when it was no longer possible.

This universal struggle involves more than knowing to what extent one should use life-extending medical technology. It's fear that I see in the eyes of my patients and their family members: the fear of saying good-bye, the fear that this life is all that there is, and the fear that they'll never see each other again. At times, however, something extraordinary happens. This book is about those extraordinary times.

INTRODUCTION

I was recently talking with a colleague who teaches ethics at Loyola Marymount University. She was about to begin a class on death and dying, and we were discussing end-of-life issues, such as the controversy surrounding artificial nutrients and terminally ill and brain-dead patients. With our cutting-edge technology, how does one determine when life should end?

In that moment, I recalled a patient who had experienced a deathbed vision. Then I thought about all the patients, all the deathbed visions, and all the discussions I've had over the years with colleagues. At hospice, palliative-care, and other end-of-life conferences, it was the kind of thing that was never mentioned. The experts were far too focused and serious, and had only one point of view. But after a long day of lectures, people would eventually start opening up about the patients who were behind the studies and reports presented earlier. After a drink or two over dinner, someone would recount a patient's deathbed vision, and another person would have a similar story. Suddenly, the whole group would fall into an animated discussion about who and what we see before we die.

I knew that when I brought up the phenomenon of deathbed visions, this highly respected, well-credentialed professor would have a strong reaction one way or another. Of course, my guess was that she would dismiss it, saying something like: "I'm not into all that—this is a *serious* program." But her reaction was the opposite: "It's so rarely written about, let alone discussed in a formal classroom setting. Everyone has these stories, although no one seems willing to put them down on paper."

At that time, I had deadlines looming for two books that I hadn't even started. It dawned on me that this subject would, and should, take center stage in one of them. Although that seed of an idea ultimately blossomed into the book you're currently holding in your hands, I had no idea of the journey I'd be taking as I wrote it.

During my research, I became fascinated by the richness of the topic as well as the lack of practical, credible information available. But how would I present this subject matter? What purpose would it serve? I've always felt that a valuable book needs a great purpose. My thoughts were interrupted when the phone rang. My friend Barbara was on the line, and she sounded distraught. She'd just returned from visiting her 92-year-old mother, who was healthy enough but was experiencing the usual problems that come with old age. Barbara shared how hard it was to watch her mother slowly deteriorate, and then she told me that a close friend's parent had recently died. "I don't understand why I'm so depressed," she said. "I've faced loss before."

Barbara had been through a lot. She'd volunteered in hospice; she'd lived through the Vietnam era; and then during the AIDS crisis, she'd watched as so many of her friends had died all at once.

"The past is different," I replied. "Vietnam was a war, and you were on the front lines when the AIDS epidemic broke out."

She agreed. This *was* different for her—and for all of us. Just as our parents are older, we are older, too. The sudden death that we expected as young people was now transforming into a slow-motion deterioration of our own bodies. Instead of "live fast, die young," many of us baby boomers are currently facing a natural progression in living and dying. Barbara was zeroing in on it when she asked, "Is there nothing to look forward to? Is this it? Just suffering and death?"

I told her that death was inevitable; suffering, however, was optional. Yet there was more to it than that. I listened to her words, but I also heard what was underneath. I asked, "Are you feeling hopeless?"

That was indeed the issue . . . and Barbara began to sob. If she had 500 tears to cry, I said, she shouldn't stop at 300. When she called the next day to let me know she was feeling better, I realized why I wanted to write this book and what it's truly about.

A Book about Hope

Although I lost my mother too soon, my father remained an incredible optimist his whole life, even when he was dying. I was busy trying to make sure he was comfortable and pain free, and at first didn't notice that he had become very sad. He told me how much he was going to miss me once he was gone. And then he mentioned how much he was saying good-bye to: his loved ones, his favorite foods, the sky, the outdoors, and a million other things of this world. He was overcome by sadness I could not (and would not) take away from him.

My father was very down for the next few days. But then one morning he told me that my mother, his wife, *had come to him the night before*. "I was looking at all I was losing, and I'd forgotten that I was going to be with her again. I'm going to see her soon," he said. He looked at me as if he realized I would still remain here. Then he added, "We'll be there waiting for you." Over the next two days, his demeanor changed dramatically. He had gone from a hopeless dying man with only death in front of him to a hopeful man who was going to be reunited with the love of his life. My father lived with hope . . . and also died with it.

As someone who has spent most of my life writing, teaching, and working with the dying, I can't prove to you that my father's vision was real. I can only talk about my experience as a son and about countless other occurrences that take place every day. I used to believe that the only thing we needed to alleviate was the suffering of the dying by providing good pain management and symptom control. I know now that we have more than opiates for pain, and we have more than anti-anxiety medication to combat fear and distress. We have the "who" and "what" we see before we die, which is perhaps the greatest comfort to the dying.

My wish is that you'll find the hope that my father did—the hope I felt after hearing his story. This is the same hope that so many patients and family members feel when they've experienced these visions.

So that is what this book is about: *hope*. Hope that there is more. Hope that we don't watch each other slowly die and then simply wait for our own deaths. We want to hope that there is a heaven, that some part of us doesn't die, so we can be reunited with those we love and maybe even with religious figures who've inspired us in our lives.

Throughout my years of working with the dying, their visions of visits from loved ones who have already died are only the first of three commonly shared experiences that remain beyond our ability to explain and fully understand. The second type is getting ready for a trip. The notion of the dying preparing for a journey isn't new or unusual. Although, interestingly enough, it's always referring to an earthly journey. People talk about packing their bags or looking for their tickets—they don't mention chariots descending from heaven or traveling to eternity in some other manner. The archetype is about life and transitions, not endings. The saying "It's not about the destination, but the journey" has never rung more true than here.

The third type is known as "crowded rooms." The dying often talk about their room being filled with other people. The word I hear over and over again is *crowded.* It's not unusual for the dying to recognize some but not all of these visitors. We will look into who these people are and the connections they have during both life and death. By doing so, the very idea that we die alone may be challenged. What if the journey at the end of life is not a lonely path into eternity, but rather, an incredible reunion with those we have loved and lost? Beyond that, what if the dying hold a connection to those who have been long forgotten? What could that offer to the living?

How This Book Is Set Up

The following chapters will bring about new insights and ideas on what the end of life looks like and the miraculous encounters that are put before us. This book follows my exploration into the deathbed phenomenon. Just like when I started researching, it begins by taking a look at the definition of the term *deathbed vision* and what it means. Since I have experience in the medical field, I was curious to see if this subject was acknowledged or touched on in other areas and professions. As I searched, I was pleasantly surprised to discover quite a bit of discourse in the legal world concerning the veracity of a dying person's final words. I've also examined the role that deathbed visions play in the arts. All of my findings are included here.

Of course, the majority of this book is made up of the personal stories told by numerous health-care professionals, and I've divided them into several chapters. (Throughout many of these chapters, you'll find my thoughts and commentary in italics in order to set them apart from the stories.) All of these witnesses have generously shared their personal experiences. I've done my best to retain their voices on these pages, and I'm excited to present their amazing accounts here.

In "Visions of the Dying: Part I," I wanted to know if doctors and nurses had stories about deathbed visions from their patients and if they were willing to share them. They did, and they were! Encouraged by those powerful accounts, I checked in with many mental-health professionals (such as social workers, psychologists, and counselors) to see if *they* might want to discuss their experiences with the dying. The results were incredible, and their accounts are in the chapter titled "Visions of the Dying: Part II." The accounts here are only a sampling of what these individuals see on a daily basis, and for each story included in these pages, there are countless more just like it.

I also think that any book dealing with such extraordinary events must take a look at spiritual and religious visions as shared by members of the clergy as well as families. I've included many of their inspiring, heartwarming stories herein. Finally, in the last chapters of the book, I explore the other aspects of deathbed visions that I've described: the *trips* that the dying prepare for, and the *crowded rooms* that many see in their last moments on Earth.

My hope—my "great purpose" for this book—is to begin a conversation, a continuing dialogue for health-care professionals to discuss more than *who* died, but *how* they died; and for families and friends to take a deeper look at their loved ones' final days with open minds and hearts.

Everyone should be able to talk openly about what they see and feel at the end of life without fear of what others may think. I invite you to reflect on the stories often told behind closed doors, and only after all of the guests have left. As I've looked back on the many patients I've been with as they died and remembered their deathbed visions, I've realized that in each case, the vision brought hope to the dying person and to his or her family. It gave them a different way to view death. In the final analysis, one thing is clear to me: *life ends, but love is eternal.*

CHAPTER ONE

DEATHBED VISIONS UP CLOSE

"It's very beautiful over there."
— final words of Thomas Edison

It's not unusual for the dying to have visions of someone who has already passed on, yet it's interesting to note that such a comforting phenomenon doesn't seem to appear in other frightening situations . . . where death is not likely. For example, there are no documented cases of people being visited by deceased family members when they're stuck in an elevator. And loved ones long gone don't seem to show up to help when a person is lost on a hike. Yes, there are stories of visions and angels comforting and guiding individuals in extreme situations, but only when death is imminent.

I spend much of my days in at least three hospitals and a hospice, and you just don't hear these stories from patients who are ill but *not* dying. With very few exceptions, these visions only occur when someone is clearly close to death.

Moreover, the visions people experience at the end of life are remarkably similar. For example, the dying are most often visited by a mother or mother figure. It shouldn't be too surprising that the person who is actually present as we cross the threshold of life and take our first breath once again appears at the threshold as we take our *last* breath.

Hands passionately reaching upward to some unseen force is witnessed in many deathbed encounters. One person, for instance, recently shared that her father, who had cancer, was barely alive after a second cardiac arrest he'd had in the hospital. He was connected to every machine possible, and had a tube in his nose and another down his throat that enabled him to breathe. Suddenly, he lifted both arms up in the air, stretching and seemingly reaching toward something.

The daughter quickly showed the nurse, who responded by explaining that patients are always trying to pull their tubes out. Although the daughter pointed out that her father wasn't touching his nose or mouth, or any of the other tubes surrounding him, the nurse continued to turn a deaf ear and increased the patient's level of sedation. The daughter, of course, felt that something significant had occurred.

Are Visions Proof of the Afterlife?

The health-care system bears witness, but how does it actually regard the phenomena of deathbed visions? Is it accepted and formally discussed and written about, or does it exist on the fringe? In their last hours or moments on Earth, how are the patients who have deathbed visions viewed? Those outside of hospice and end-of-life-care medical establishments have long minimized and discounted the experiences of the dying; and they often attribute deathbed visions to pain medication, fever, or lack of oxygen to the brain. Discounting a patient's experience has probably been around as long as the dying have had visions.

William James, who was a professor at Harvard from 1872 to 1907 as well as a lecturer at numerous universities, is often referred to as "the father of American psychology." Yet in his lifetime, he was ridiculed for forming The American

Society for Psychical Research. Unfortunately, we have a long-standing practice of criticizing those who look outside the traditional medical box.

While at the bedside of my patients, I often suggest to family members that there's no point in telling their father that he's hallucinating, or that Joseph is dead and can't possibly be here in the room. For all we know, the veil that separates life and death is lifted in the last moments of life, and those who are dying may be more in touch with that world than with ours.

Instead of denying a patient's reality, I respond by asking questions: "What is your loved one saying? Can you describe what else you see?" Perhaps a deceased family member is telling the patient that it's okay to die, or maybe they're reminiscing about growing up together. I've heard people tell their dying loved ones: "It's great that Betty is here," or "I knew that Mother would come to meet you," or "I'm so glad Jeff is with you now."

If you find the concept of a dead loved one greeting you on your deathbed impossible or ridiculous, consider what I finally realized as a parent: You protect your children from household dangers. You hold their hands when they cross the street on their first day of school. You take care of them when they have the flu, and you see them through as many milestones as you can. Now fast-forward 70 years or after you yourself have passed away. What if there really is an afterlife and you receive a message that your son or daughter will be dying soon? If you were allowed to go to your child, wouldn't you?

Deathbed Visions vs. Near-Death Experiences

Deathbed visions are also known by other names, including *near-death awareness, deathbed phenomena,* and *death-related sensory experiences.* They are different from *near-death experiences,* in which a person survives clinical death. While deathbed visions often involve a deceased messenger who appears days or moments before death, near-death experiences are out-of-body "journeys" by individuals who recall seeing light, a tunnel, and/or have an opportunity to review their lives. People usually pass on shortly after deathbed visions, whereas those who have near-death experiences survive and recount what they saw. This book focuses on the deathbed visions, trips, and crowded-rooms phenomena that the dying experience in their last days and hours on Earth.

In terms of the overall ways in which society views what cannot be easily understood or proven, there may be an unintended arrogance in the judgment of the visions presented here. Most of us think that we already know everything, and if there's something outside our knowledge, a practical explanation must exist. We ask ourselves, *If deceased loved ones* _really_ *do appear to the dying, why can't we, the healthy ones, see them?* I believe that *if* there's a power that lowers the veil between life and death, why wouldn't it also have the ability to lift the veil and choose to reveal itself to certain individuals?

In my first book, *The Needs of the Dying,* I shared a story that I think says it all about the dead only appearing to those who are dying:

> Roberta lay at death's door going in and out of consciousness while her daughter, Audrey, sat attentively by her bed. Suddenly, Roberta whispered, "My mother

is here. Audrey, your grandmother is here . . . she is so beautiful."

Audrey glanced at the foot of her mother's bed and looked around the room. "Mom, where is she? I don't see her!" she responded frantically.

The dying woman turned abruptly to her daughter, as if withdrawing from the vision of her own dead mother, and replied sternly, "Of course *you* can't see her—she's here for me, not you!"

Her daughter understood the message.

More Than a Hallucination?

"There are some remarkable instances where the dying person, before the moment of transition from earth, appears to see and recognize some of his deceased relatives or friends," wrote Sir William F. Barrett in *On the Threshold of the Unseen* in 1918. However, he added, "One cannot always attach much to this evidence. . . ." Barrett labeled the experiences as hallucinations. Despite medicine brushing these encounters aside, deathbed visions continued to be reported. Even Barrett, a distinguished physicist, began viewing these episodes as more than hallucinations and eventually became one of the principal founders of the Society for Psychical Research.

The dying being visited by deceased relatives is often a theme in the end-of-life narrative. While this archetype has been around a long time, it first appeared in scientific literature in 1924 in an article written once again by Sir William Barrett, while he was a physics professor at the Royal College of Science in Dublin. This article was unique in that it contained an interesting story that could not be explained.

Barrett's wife, an obstetrician, was called into the operating room to deliver the child of "Doris M." The infant was healthy; however, Doris began massively hemorrhaging. As she lay dying, the doctor was shocked to realize that the woman was having an otherworldly vision. Afterward, the doctor recounted the experience to her husband:

> "Oh, lovely, lovely," [Doris M.] said.
> [Barrett's wife] asked, "What is lovely?"
> "What I *see*," she replied in low, intense tones.
> "What do you see?"
> "Lovely brightness—wonderful beings."

Doris was transfixed by what she saw. She then seemed to have even more focus and clarity:

> "Why, it's father! Oh, he's so glad I'm coming; he *is* so glad. It would be perfect if only W. [her husband] would come too."
> Her baby was brought for her to see. She looked at it with interest, and then asked, "Do you think I ought to stay for baby's sake?" Then turning towards the vision again, she said, "I can't—I can't stay; if you could see what I do, you would know I can't stay. . . ."
> She spoke to her father, saying, "I am coming," turning at the same time to look at me, saying, "Oh, he is so near." On looking at the same place again, she said with a rather puzzled expression, "He has Vida with him, Vida is with him." Then she said, "You do want me, Dad; I am coming."

William Barrett was at first skeptical of his wife's story but was soon convinced of its accuracy once he learned the significance of Doris's sister, Vida, appearing with her father. Evidently, Vida had died three weeks earlier, but that information had been withheld from the expectant mother. Barrett wrote that he had considered whether this vision was a hallucination, but there was no explanation for Doris's puzzlement when she saw her sister, Vida (whom she thought to be alive), with her father.

These types of stories were slowly gaining awareness in the medical world. In nonmedical writings, however, the "transition to another world" was common in deathbed scenes. And, of course, the idea that birth is not a beginning and death is not an ending was an ever-present message in religious writings—but it hadn't yet found a legitimate place in medicine.

Even the 1924 article featuring Doris's deathbed vision isn't the first to introduce an unexplainable twist into the patient narrative. Hensleigh Wedgwood, who wrote for *The Spectator*, a British newspaper circa 1711, tells a very similar story:

> A young girl, a near connection of mine, was dying of consumption. She had lain for some days in a poor condition, taking no notice of anything, when she opened her eyes and, looking upwards, said slowly, "Susan—and Jane—and Ellen!" She was recognizing the presence of her three sisters, who had previously died of the same disease. Then, after a short pause, she said, "And Edward, too!" She was naming a brother who was supposed to be alive and well in India, as if surprised at seeing him in their company. She said no more and died shortly afterwards and letters came from India two weeks later, announcing that Edward had had an accident and died.

◆◇◆

History has often treated the words of the dying as reality, but the majority of medical professionals wouldn't entertain such a notion, which eventually made me curious to find out where deathbed visions were viewed differently (and by whom). I was encouraged by all that I was learning and knew from the regularity by which they were appearing that I should continue to search.

The next area I'd explore on my journey was how the legal world perceived the words of the dying. Would this information prove to be intriguing and shed new light on this mysterious line of inquiry? I was more than ready to find out.

CHAPTER TWO

BELIEVING
THE WORDS
OF THE DYING

"I still live."
— final words of Daniel Webster

Someone once told me that maturity is when you accept the fact that two contradictory ideas can exist together. For instance, community service can be a selfless and generous act, or it can be used for self-aggrandizement. It can be very interesting when two contradicting ideas actually exist at the same time in one person, especially when you mix this concept with the principle that things change when observed—we know it depends on the situation and who is doing the observing.

Deathbed visions are no exception. At the core, they are statements made by the dying that will or won't be believed, but most visions experienced in a person's last moments are not taken seriously or considered credible by those around them. Yet when we look at deathbed declarations from a legal standpoint, we may find a completely different point of view. I am by no means a lawyer, but the information I was able to obtain after consulting a university professor and a couple of attorneys is fascinating in terms of the dying. I present it for your consideration so that you have a complete picture of the ways in which we respond to what a person says moments before death.

Let's first take a look at the story of William, someone I grew up with.

◆

William's mother, Jennifer, didn't seem to have a vision before she died, but she did make a statement that would remain a mystery for years to come. William was just ten years old when his mother, who battled kidney disease for much of his life, began to take a turn for the worse.

William's father, Jeffrey, a strong, stoic, powerful attorney, had brought his legal background to his son's upbringing. If William said something that wasn't "concrete," his father would respond: "I would never present that to a jury." For instance, if he stated, "I heard that two kids were sent home from school for fighting," his dad would quickly cut him off, saying, "That would never be allowed in a court of law. You have to have direct knowledge."

As Jennifer's health deteriorated, William's dad focused on practical concerns by making sure her affairs were in order and by speaking to various doctors, ensuring that every option for treatment was being explored and implemented. When her condition worsened, she was hospitalized. Jeffrey was aware that children under 14 weren't permitted to visit patients, but never commented on it. Sometimes William would get to see his mom, but usually he wouldn't.

William never brought up the rule to his dad. He wouldn't dare say that the rule was unfair because he knew his father would treat the topic matter-of-factly, comparing it to some law in an instant. He imagined that his father's response would be: "It's the rule and you should always obey it, even when a nurse decides to break it for your sake."

When his mother was a few days away from death, not really communicating much anymore, William was able to visit her and stood by her bedside. At one point, she glanced up and saw him, and then looked forward as if she were going to address someone (or maybe herself). Then she said, "Sorry about March 16."

William immediately thought, *March 16? That's my birthday! What does that mean?* It was a question that would haunt him for years.

After she died, William frequently thought about his mother's statement, since he never fully understood what she meant. He didn't feel comfortable discussing it with his father, who wasn't much of a grieving guy. William knew that his dad was sad, and Jeffrey knew that his son was sad, but they never talked about their feelings.

When William was about 17, he was trying to figure out how to use a photograph-developing kit. He laid out all of the solutions and wondered if he'd actually end up with a clear picture from a blank piece of paper. For some reason, he began to think about his mother's statement all those years before. Maybe he could finally talk to his father about it. It certainly wasn't concrete, but perhaps the fact that it happened was all the evidence he needed. Maybe the story didn't need to be as fully developed as his picture.

William looked down and saw an image appearing as he added the solutions. He let the photograph dry, thinking that he'd show it to his dad later and bring up the topic of his mother's deathbed declaration. Once his father came home, William showed him the photo, explaining that he'd developed it himself with a kit.

His father looked at it for a while, and then said, "It's not a great picture. You should never show something that isn't your best work. I certainly wouldn't present this to a jury," and he handed it back to his son. Needless to say, William decided not to mention his mom's deathbed declaration. He could practically hear his father quickly dismissing it.

Unfortunately, his dad would die five years later of a heart attack, and William never told him about his mother's final words. Yet just a few years later, when William was 25, he found himself at his aunt Mona's deathbed and caught a break in the mystery.

William sat there quietly studying his aunt's face, thinking about how much she resembled his mother. Suddenly, Mona's face became animated as she woke up and saw her nephew sitting there. Without thinking, he blurted out, "When Mom was dying, she told me that she was sorry about March 16. That's my birthday."

His aunt replied, "Your mother had a child when she was very young. We all knew about it." That was all she said—in fact, she didn't speak another word while he was there, and passed away the next day. William was perplexed but glad to have another piece of the story. He knew *this* was the conversation he was meant to have—not the one with his deceased attorney father, who would have needed all the facts.

William told his aunt's daughter, his cousin Sylvia, who was a nurse administrator, the entire story. She said, "One day at work they were giving a presentation about the history of the hospital. From the first day I started, I always thought the place felt familiar. I learned that it was once a home for unwed mothers and realized that I had been there as a little girl to visit my aunt Jennifer, your mother."

Noting her cousin's confusion, Sylvia asked, "Don't you get it? You have a sibling out there! Your mom had to give up her child for adoption when she was a teenager. It's not like today—she had no choice. The family must have felt tremendous shame and sent her away to secretly have the baby."

William contacted an organization that did work on behalf of parents and children trying to find their biological relatives. A few weeks later, someone from the agency called and said, "We found your sibling's birth records. You have a brother who was born on March 16—"

William jumped in, exclaiming, "That's my birthday!"

"It's also your brother's," the woman stated.

Finally, William knew what his mother's dying declaration meant. He eventually tracked down his brother and wondered if his father would have been proud of him for doing his "best work" and having the complete picture. Could he now present this information to a hypothetical jury?

William did not know that deathbed declarations are often presumed to be the truth in a court of law, and viewing them through a legal lens creates a completely different story and outcome. In terms of the legal system, a dying declaration is a statement made by a dying person that's most often used in deciding a murder case. In Western medicine, these "declarations" or utterances, especially a statement involving an otherworldly vision, are not considered valid.

The law doesn't comment specifically on whether the dying see visions. However, it often does consider a dying person's words as the truth, especially when it comes to murder. The idea is that individuals who are fully aware that they're moments away from death have reason to be completely honest, perhaps much more so than they ever did before. Even with the argument that a dying person might be retaliating or accusing the wrong person of a crime, the law still often favors deathbed declarations as the truth.

This law, which originated in medieval English courts, ascribed to the principle of *Nemo moriturus praesumitur mentiri*, meaning "a dying person is not presumed to lie." An early example was in the 12th century when dying declarations, such as deathbed statements, were already long understood to hold a "special trust." Typical reasoning at the time for such an admission was expressed by Lord Chief Justice Mansfield, who indicated that the dying declaration of Lady Jane Douglas was admissible, for "would she have died with a lie in her mouth . . . ?" (On her deathbed, Lady Douglas had insisted that she was the birth mother of her son, Archibald, which would make him the legal heir to her brother, a wealthy duke.)

Even today, centuries later, the legality of a dying declaration exception still stands. Therefore, a dying person's last words regarding a crime are exempt from the "Hearsay" rule, which usually prohibits the use of a statement made by someone other than the person who uses it to testify during a trial because of the inherent untrustworthiness of hearsay. For example, if one of Nicole Brown Simpson's friends had heard Nicole say, "I think O.J. is so mad he's going to kill me," that may be ruled by the court as hearsay. However, if she had been found dying and said, "O.J. stabbed me," that would have fallen under the "Hearsay Rule Exception."

To better understand this, we must examine *hearsay*, a statement made out of court that is offered in the courtroom as evidence to prove the truth of the matter asserted. The judge or jury must determine whether evidence offered as proof is credible. Three evidentiary rules help the judge or jury determine this:

1. Before being allowed to testify, witnesses must swear that their testimony is truthful. This is done with a Bible along with reciting the words *so help me God*.

2.   Witnesses must be physically present at the trial in order for the judge or jury to observe the testimony firsthand. For example, did they look like they were telling the truth? What were their body movements like? Their facial expressions? What might the jury or judge observe besides the spoken words?

3.   Witnesses are subject to cross-examinations by any party who did not call the witness to testify. A lawyer may wish to ask for more details, for instance, such as the time of day and the lighting conditions. Does the witness have a motive to lie?

All evidence used in the U.S. legal system must conform to the Federal Rules of Evidence, which prohibits most statements made outside a courtroom from being used as evidence in court. Out-of-court statements hinder the ability of the judge or jury to probe testimony for inaccuracies caused by ambiguity, insincerity, faulty perception, or erroneous memory. Thus, statements made out of court are perceived as untrustworthy.

If the person who made the dying declaration had the slightest hope of recovery, no matter how unreasonable, the statement is *not* admissible into evidence. A dying declaration is usually introduced by the prosecution, but can be used on behalf of the accused.

It is crucial that the person believe that he or she is dying in order for the dying declaration to remain legally pure. Some paramedics, in an effort to be compassionate and hopeful, unknowingly have said things like: "You're going to be okay" or "You're going to make it." The trouble is that if the dying person believes there is a chance of survival, the declaration is no longer valid. For this reason, many paramedics are instructed as to how to take and record dying statements.

The dying declaration exception of the Federal Rules of Evidence is as follows:

> Rule 804(b)(2) of the Federal Rules of Evidence states the position that the Dying Declaration enjoys a special position within the law of evidence.
>
> Rule 804. Hearsay Exceptions; Declarant Unavailable [Obviously, the dying cannot go to court.]
>
> (b) Hearsay exceptions.—The following are not excluded by the hearsay rule if the declarant is unavailable as a witness:
>
> (2) Statement under belief of impending death.—In a prosecution for homicide or in a civil action or proceeding, a statement made by a declarant while believing that the declarant's death was imminent, concerning the cause or circumstances of what the declarant believed to be impending death.

Even Shakespeare said that the declarant, being at the point of death, "must lose the use of all deceit."

The law sides with the dying on the basis of three concepts:

1. There is no longer any self-serving purpose to be furthered.

2. If a belief exists in a punishment soon to be inflicted by a Higher Power upon human ill-doing, the fear of this punishment will outweigh any possible motive for deception, and will actually counterbalance the inclination to gratify a possible spirit of revenge.

3.   Even without such a belief, there is a natural and instinctive awe at the approach of an unknown future—a physical revulsion common to all men, irresistible, and independent of theological belief.

The same arguments are presented against deathbed visions (medical) and dying declarations (legal), yet with different outcomes. Here we are looking at the same argument regarding lack of oxygen to the brain and coming up with different conclusions about the dying speaking of visions or making specific declarations. According to traditional Western medicine, a dying person's last words are usually not considered as the truth: in the legal world, the dying are presumed, under the law, to be telling the truth.

The Supreme Court has been interested in the "trustworthiness" of the dying declaration. In *Mattox v. United States,* the Court addressed the issue of whether admission of dying declarations was constitutional under the confrontation clause of the sixth amendment. The Court held that the admission of these statements was constitutional, and noted that dying declarations:

> From time immemorial . . . have been treated as competent testimony, and no one would have the hardihood at this day to question their admissibility. . . . The sense of impending death is presumed to remove all temptation to falsehood, and to enforce as strict an adherence to the truth as would the obligation of an oath.

Deathbed visions will continue to be part of the process of dying, even though we will never be able to prove (or disprove) them. The legal system has set a clear precedence for *believing* the words of the dying. As I continued my exploration, I wondered, *Will the medical community ever reach this consensus? Are dying individuals not to be believed if they claim that they see their deceased father, but believed if they say that they witnessed their neighbor murdering their father?*

I found myself hoping that medical health-care providers would become more aware of the credibility these statements hold in a court of law. After all, if our legal system could view these statements with such reverence, why couldn't the doctors and nurses at a dying patient's bedside also do so? I decided to go directly to the source in the next part of my journey.

CHAPTER THREE

VISIONS
OF THE DYING

Part I

"Too kind, too kind."
— final words of Florence Nightingale

Now let's take a close look at the deathbed visions that nurses and doctors have shared with me. Some are from events that took place with their patients, and others are stories they've actually gone through with their own families. The nurses and doctors featured here aren't just from hospice facilities; they also represent many different areas of medicine, including ICU and oncology. Some experienced these visions when they were novices, but for others, it happened much later in their careers.

•◇•

A Family Affair

by Heather

I've worked in the medical field for years as a nurse. I try to know the ins and outs of the health-care system, but nothing challenges a person as much as when his or her own family members become ill.

My mother, Mabel, and I were out on a Saturday afternoon. By the time we'd finished our errands and had driven back to my parents' house, it was nightfall. We were both surprised by the sudden darkness and then remembered that we'd just turned back the clocks the night before. As I brought in a grocery bag, I called out for my dad, Joseph, to hold the door open, but there was no response. My mother and I looked at each another, wondering what was up. I started to put away the food while Mom went to look for Dad, whom she was sure must be napping in front of the TV. She found the TV on, but no Joseph. She checked all the rooms and both the back and front yards, but he was nowhere to be found.

Mom called a few neighbors, who hadn't seen him. After an hour, we were both pretty panicked. At the age of 85, my father had stopped driving due to his failing eyesight, and we were afraid that he had attempted to drive. Although we were quickly relieved to see that the car was still in the garage, we couldn't imagine where he had gone or why. Our concern deepened when we saw his wallet sitting on the dresser.

Mother called the police, and I drove around the neighborhood searching. Four frantic hours later, we got a call that an officer had found my father across town, and that he seemed confused and wasn't sure where he was. The next few days were filled with doctors' appointments to confirm what we suspected: Dad had Alzheimer's.

My mom, of course, had realized that her husband was getting older, but when she noticed the odd little things he did, she'd say, "No one in their 80s is a rocket scientist." Even so, she never expected him to wander away and forget where he lived. After the diagnosis, we found ways to make sure he was never alone and even replaced the locks so that you needed keys to get in and out of the house when we were sleeping. Family and friends also pitched in during the day if my mom had to go out and I was working.

As if things weren't hard enough, my mother began to have stomach problems and was feeling very fatigued. Now I was dealing with two elderly parents in declining health. On top of my father having Alzheimer's, Mom was diagnosed with pancreatic cancer. I soon found that juggling my job as a nurse and caring for my own children as well as my ailing parents was more than I could handle (and quitting work wasn't an option). My co-workers had been mentioning for a while that perhaps it was time to put my dad in a facility; and even though I'd resisted the idea at first, it now seemed like my options were dwindling.

So my parents and I began looking at nursing homes and found Sunset Gardens, which was a really nice place. Dad was content, as this facility had a perfect mixture of comfort and security. After all, he was still a strong man in otherwise good health. It was a blessing that the move was surprisingly uneventful. Mom was more upset about living apart from her husband, so when she wasn't at her own doctors' appointments, she was there at Sunset Gardens with him.

At 81 years old, my mother decided not to undergo chemo or other aggressive treatments, preferring to let nature take it course. The doctors told her that she probably had a year or so, but no one expected her to suddenly fall on the way to the bathroom one day and break her hip. After a lengthy hospital stay, *she* now required around-the-clock care. Since her needs were different from my dad's, however, she ended up in a separate facility. I was now shuttling between my kids' school, my job, and two nursing homes.

For my mom, things quickly went from bad to worse: after the broken hip came a urinary-tract infection, then a respiratory infection. As her illnesses escalated, I was getting over to see my father less and less. Other family members would make sure he had a visit at least two or three times a week, even though at this point he was no longer recognizing loved ones.

Mom's doctors met with us and explained that there were just too many things going wrong with her body at once, yet returning to the hospital for more testing didn't make sense. While we agreed, we ultimately left the decision to Mom. She said, "I've lived over eight decades. I can't complain too much—it's just my time."

I was searching for a way for my parents to be together, but my mother's facility didn't accept Alzheimer's patients, while my father's *only* accepted patients with Alzheimer's and dementia. We were unsure if we should even tell him how bad Mom was doing because there was basically nothing he could do. We'd hoped to find a way to get him out for a few hours to see his wife when the call came that Mom's condition had worsened: her blood pressure was dropping, and her heart rate was increasing.

That evening, my family and I sat by my mom, who was still very alert, but her breathing was more audible than usual. She suddenly looked up and said, "Joseph died. Why didn't anyone tell me this?"

I jumped in and quickly corrected her: "Mom, Daddy isn't dead. He's still in the nursing home."

Startled by her statement, I suddenly realized that I'd better find a way to get Dad over here. We were afraid that my mom was beginning to lose her faculties, and we wanted her to see her husband while she could still talk to him.

"Mom," I said, "we'll see if the nursing home will let us pick up Dad so he can visit." I nodded to my cousin Jackie to call the nursing home to make arrangements for one of us to get him.

"Joseph already came to say good-bye," Mom insisted, "and he told me that I'd be with him soon."

We all just looked at each other, acknowledging that my mother was hallucinating. I gently repeated, "Mom, Dad is in the nursing home. We're going to bring him here."

Once again she repeated, "No, he's dead," but this time, she also sat up. "Look, there he is!" She seemed to be gazing past everybody, and then she said, "Joseph, you came back for me." Her eyes filled with tears, and she lay back on the bed.

Just then, a nurse and my cousin motioned for me to come over and talk to them at the nurses' station. I met them just outside the door when Jackie said, "Heather, I don't know how to tell you this. I called the nursing home, and Joseph died about 15 minutes ago. He had a heart attack."

Mom died two days later. Even though I hadn't seen the vision of my father, I found great comfort in the fact that he had come to my mother, and now they were together again. Since my parents are gone, I rarely tell this story, but it feels as if I went from a medical nightmare to the universe stepping in, allowing Mom and Dad to pass away peacefully with each other. I admit that it's beyond my understanding, but I believe I had a special glimpse into a world rarely seen.

•◈•

WHAT IS IT?

by Nathan

As a new nurse in the 1980s, I learned firsthand that death doesn't always occur in the ways we would expect. I realized that we are immortal beings having a mortal experience.

I was working in a large nursing home in New York on the 3 P.M. to 11 P.M. shift, and as is too often the case in facilities of this size, the staff always wished for more time with each patient.

Well, here it was late into the evening, and I'd already finished feeding, bathing, and helping my patients get comfortable in their beds for the night. Suddenly, I heard an eerie moan from down the hall that sounded like: "Noooo, noooo." I immediately recognized the deep voice as my patient Frank, an affable, elderly gentleman with a little bit of confusion. I went straight to his room and found him sitting up in bed. He was rattling the bed rails, and his hands reached toward the sky as he wailed, "Noooo, noooo!"

"What is it, Frank?" I asked.

He stopped staring toward the ceiling and looked down, as if he were withdrawing from one place and coming into another. He looked me directly in the eyes and said with urgency, "I gotta go—it's time!"

Well, being the good nurse that I am, I got him to the bathroom as fast as I could! He kind of cooperated to some extent but was very agitated. I checked the bed to see if he'd had an accident, but the sheets were clean. In the next moment, I heard the IV of the patient next to him beeping. I didn't want to leave Frank, but I had to check on the other patient in case it was something serious. Frank looked firmly planted on the toilet, but I strapped him in, just in case, to prevent him from falling.

As I was finishing working with the other patient's IV, I heard that same, "Noooo, noooo! I gotta go!"

I ran back to Frank, where he was still safely sitting on the toilet. As I apologized for having briefly left him, he came out of the daze somewhat. He was looking up at the ceiling again, repeating his urgent statement about needing to go. I thought he was finished using the bathroom, so I unstrapped him from the safety harness and was getting ready to move him back to bed.

In that moment, he reached up, stared at the ceiling, and repeated, "Noooo, noooo!"

"What is it, Frank?" I knew he wasn't hallucinating; he was clearly seeing something.

"Death has come to get me," he finally replied. "The angel of death is here."

I don't know what inspired me, but I asked, "Well, is anyone else there?"

He looked at me with a puzzled expression, but then shifted his gaze back to the ceiling. He tilted his head and smiled, saying, "Oh, the angels of heaven are here, too." As he stood up on shaky legs, I rushed in to support him, noting how light he felt as his entire body strained upward. Frank raised his arms in the air, fully extending every finger as if he were trying to touch the ceiling. Then he dropped heavily into my arms and died.

I still get a chill when I remember that moment. I witnessed a person become almost weightless and then deadweight in a single instant. In fact, Frank became so heavy that I couldn't lift him onto his bed. Instead, I gently sat him back down on the toilet and pushed the emergency call button because I didn't know what else to do.

While I waited, the head nurse arrived and checked his vitals. We confirmed that he had expired right then and there, but I never told my supervisor what Frank had said nor what I believed had happened. I was afraid she'd think I was crazy! I was also embarrassed to admit that I'd misinterpreted a request to go to heaven as a request to go to the bathroom.

Now, some 30 years later, I feel privileged that I got to witness a person experiencing something beyond what most of us can normally see.

THE KISS

by Nina

I was in my early 30s and had been married for six years. My husband and I had two kids: a three-year-old boy and a four-year-old girl. As a nurse who also went to law school, I successfully moved from bedside care to hospital administration as a health-care attorney. At the same time, I was trying to balance being a wife and mother.

I thought I had it all. My husband was a Realtor, which was helpful for us since he could rearrange his daytime schedule more easily than I could in order to help with the children. I really thought our family life was on track and just like everyone else's . . . until one day my husband told me that he was in love with another woman and wanted a divorce. (His reasoning was that we'd gotten married too young and weren't truly in love with each other.)

I was overwhelmed by emotions about how my life was going to change; and after the divorce, I found myself in the midst of a real juggling act. The kids were in day care, and my world was getting more demanding. The real-estate market wasn't doing all that great, so I was making more money than my ex-husband. Now it was my sole responsibility to provide for my children, as his child-support checks only came intermittently.

As time went on, however, I got more accustomed to being a single parent. My ex-husband eventually remarried and moved out of state. From time to time, I'd think back on his comment that we'd never really been in love and realized he was right. There had been no romance between us because we were just too young.

Now that my kids were eight and nine, I wondered if I would ever find true love. I adored my family and dealt with all the challenges that came along, but I was often overwhelmed by having to do it all myself. Some of my friends made me even more concerned by remarking that my chances of finding a partner who would also be a perfect fit for my son and daughter were slim to none. I was feeling hopeless and was starting to give up on the idea that I'd find someone who'd love me *and* my kids.

Then, much to my surprise, I met a man named Bill in yoga class. From our first kiss, I knew we were meant to be, and so did he. It was like no other kiss I'd ever had. If this was love, I was sure I was feeling it deeply! Bill adored me and my children, and we eventually got married. I'd often catch myself thinking about what a wonderful man he was, and how much he loved all of us. He had also become more of a parent to my children than their own birth father.

Years later, the kids were in college, I was working, and Bill had gone on to teach yoga. He began to complain about headaches, which I paid very little attention to at first, besides suggesting he take something for it. He was reluctant to take pills but ultimately did try a few different over-the-counter remedies, all to no avail.

When Bill finally went to see a doctor, I was sure the diagnosis would be high blood pressure since it ran in his family. Maybe he was at risk for a stroke—my worst nightmare. Little did I know that there were *many* nightmares to follow when I learned that my husband's headaches were caused by a tumor near his spine that was affecting the fluid in his central nervous system.

We went to the best doctors and hospitals that Boston had to offer. I felt so fortunate to be living in a big city that had so many resources and was a leader in medical care and research . . . but as the months and treatments went by, my optimism was replaced with sadness. The flip side of living in Boston was that if a certain kind of treatment wasn't available, it meant that it probably wasn't that good anyway.

Bill spent the next several years in and out of hospitals, and the kids spent every vacation with us. I knew it was hard on them and that they'd probably rather be doing fun things with their friends, but I also could feel how much they wanted to be with Bill and me.

The kids had just gotten home for holiday break on December 22 (I'll never forget the date), and I took them to the hospital to visit Bill. When we arrived, his doctor called us all together and said, "We've tried everything, but the cancer has spread to his other organs. Bill doesn't have much time left. Would you like to take him home?"

My husband looked at me, and I looked into those beautiful eyes of his, and we just knew it was time for him to come home. That was the most special Christmas ever: no gifts—only love. For all of us, the idea of gifts seemed too painful. What on earth do you give a dying person or someone who's losing a father or husband? We had no expectations and decided to focus on the magic of the season and just being together.

A couple of days after Christmas, Bill's condition took a turn for the worse, and the doctor said we only had a few days left. This was the worst moment of my life, realizing that my husband had become so fragile. All I could do was gently rub his shoulders and give him little pecks on his cheeks.

Suddenly I realized that our small, self-contained world had a visitor . . . not from a foreign country but from heaven. At first I didn't know what to make of it when Bill started talking to someone in the room. I heard him say, "Mom, I can't believe you're here." He told her about the kids and me, as if we were being introduced, with no regard as to whether we could hear him or not. The most amazing part was that he was focusing his eyes on a particular spot, looking upward as if that was where his mother was hovering.

On the last day of his life, he talked to his mom again. Then he looked at me and said, "Come here." He gave me the most passionate kiss—the kind you have when you're dating, not when you're dying. Afterward, he told his mother, "I knew I loved her from the first kiss." And to me, he said, "To the last kiss, I love you." He died peacefully that night.

I'm Not Crazy

by Phoebe

I work as a registered nurse in palliative (end-of-life) care. I've been in the trenches with dying people for many years, but not all of my stories regarding visions come from hospital conversations.

One evening I was waiting to pick up my kids after a golf game they played with a rival school. Linda, another mom from my son's class, made some small talk with me about how much homework children have these days. Any two parents can immediately finish each other's sentences about how much school has changed from the time when they were students.

Switching gears, I asked her what she did for work.

"I'm a litigator," Linda replied.

"You get paid to argue?" I quipped. I realized right away that she must have heard that comment more times than she could remember.

"Yes, I do," she said, smiling.

"I should have been an attorney, too. I argue with doctors all day long!" When I explained to Linda that I worked in palliative care, she didn't turn and run for the hills (a lot of people do!). She wanted to know if I'd ever heard of anything unusual happening when a person died. I recalled that in my experience, the more conservative an individual appears, the less likely he or she will share a story about otherworldly visions. Although Linda appeared quite reserved, I decided to be direct: "I bet you have a story about a dying loved one who had a vision."

Instead of trying to change the subject, Linda looked around as if we were about to share a secret. Then she leaned in, and in a low voice, said, "I never told this to anyone. My aunt Rachel, who helped raise me, was 86 when she was dying. It was early in the morning, and I was the only one in the room with her. Now I'm not crazy, but it seemed like my aunt was between this world and the next—as if she were leaving the Earth plane and moving on. Then out of the blue, she said, 'Let's talk to your mom.' My mom, Juliet, had passed away six years earlier, but Aunt Rachel started having a conversation with her! I even heard my aunt say, 'I'm coming home . . . slowly, but surely.'"

The lawyer in Linda must have resurfaced because she followed up by asking, "Can you confirm that what happened to my aunt also happens to other people?"

"Yes, I can," I told her.

"Well," she said, "a lot happens that we don't appreciate until we're in the presence of someone who is dying. I happen to be a very fact-oriented person. Getting to the truth is my business, and I need facts more than I need feelings. So this experience is in contrast to who I am. I'm really *not* inclined toward this kind of story, but that doesn't make it any less true."

I nodded as she continued.

"As I get older, I find more comfort in this. I know that the occurrence had nothing to do with me and everything to do with my aunt, but having the privilege to witness someone dying is one of my more life-affirming experiences, as odd as that sounds. It has strengthened my belief that life is eternal and that we continue to exist after we die. Have you *really* heard stuff like this before?"

"Yes, I have," I answered.

"With a living person actually seeing someone from the other side?"

"Yes—in fact, deathbed visions are quite common."

"Really?!" Linda sounded surprised.

"It's true," I assured her, "but people like you don't usually talk about them."

"People like me?"

I explained that I was referring to her reluctance to share her experience, and pointed out, "You probably only told me because I work in the death-and-dying field."

"If you ever tell anyone about this, promise me that you won't use my name."

I assured her that I'd honor her request, but stressed that her story could help others. Linda smiled and said she liked that idea.

"It's too bad no one told you how common these types of visions are when your aunt was dying," I added. "Hearing someone else's story might have helped you not feel so crazy for witnessing this. Deathbed visions occur in the presence of nurses, priests, doctors—and, yes, even attorneys. That knowledge could be comforting to people."

Linda understood and was glad to let me share her story, as long as I kept my promise not to use her real name.

◆

What They Don't Teach You
in Medical School

by Jack

After graduating from medical school, I wasn't sure which branch of medicine I wanted to dedicate myself to. Then I did my oncology rotation at a hospital in Michigan and something grabbed me. Seeing patients who were so sick was difficult, but when the oncologists were able to give them more time or improve their quality of life, it was wonderful. And seeing patients in remission, going back to their everyday lives, seemed like the best kind of medicine for me. I decided that this was my calling.

It's interesting being a doctor in a family. My family still sees me just as Jack, and my medical degree doesn't give me any advantages. It's funny when your mother's home remedy beats out scientifically tested medicine. It keeps you humble and grounded.

When I went into oncology, it never occurred to me that I might see one of my own loved ones terminally ill. So when I got the news that my younger brother, Mike, who was just 41, had cancer, it was really hard for me to act like a doctor and not a saddened man who was afraid to lose his brother.

Mike was just hitting his stride; he enjoyed his career and was seeing a lot of success in his real-estate investments. It seemed incomprehensible that his cancer was advanced, and it was almost impossible for my family to face the reality that it might be too late. I tried to remain hopeful, but I knew too much.

As my brother became sicker, family and friends would turn to me for an update on his condition, but I wasn't his physician. They just assumed that I would know what to do, or think of some new way to treat him. It was strange to suddenly have the respect I'd always wanted from my family, yet this wasn't how I wanted to get it. I wanted to be the one to show the best way to heal a cut or to determine whether my nephew needed to get his tonsils removed—not to be the one to explain that Mike was dying. Watching my younger brother go through all of this was ripping me apart.

One day near the end, my mother and I were sitting with Mike, who was quiet but not sleeping. Then he suddenly started talking, as if there was someone standing right in front of him (he definitely wasn't addressing my mom or me). Mom and I looked at each other in a way that said, "What is this?"

We soon realized that Mike was indeed talking to someone, and as we listed to the conversation, it dawned on us that he was speaking to my father's parents. He had been very close to them and loved them both very much. When Grandma died, Mike started spending more time with our grandfather. Since my cousins and I were away at school, we were grateful that my brother was there and could visit him so often. After Grandpa died, it hit Mike very hard. So the notion that it was my grandparents who came to my brother as he was dying wasn't that surprising.

As a doctor, it's very easy to dismiss this sort of thing until you see it firsthand. Could my brother's vision have been a dream state? Was it a result of oxygen deprivation? A side effect of the medications? All were possible, but for my mother and me, none of those options felt right. It felt profound. Real. Neither one of us wanted to interfere, so we just observed.

For the next few hours, Mom and I watched Mike on and off in conversation. We could never quite make out exactly what he was saying, but we could hear him call both of my grandparents by name. He also had a tender, sweet look on his face. Of all the things that we were doing for him—from end-of-life care to making sure he got the best of every-thing—this "visit" seemed to bring him the most comfort.

Before this episode, there was a sense of struggle and tension in the air, but now there seemed to be only peace surrounding my brother. I truly believe that it was a result of my grandparents' visit as he died.

One family member asked me, "As a doctor, what do you make of this?" And I responded, "I don't make anything of it as a doctor. I don't have a scientific explanation. I only have my *own* experience to draw from. I took it at face value and knew it was an authentic part of the process."

When my patients have similar experiences, I don't ques-tion it as a doctor. I just accept that this is what's going on. If it feels real to a patient, so be it. But this is definitely not the kind of thing they teach in medical school.

THE ROBE

by Zack

I'm a 32-year-old who works in end-of-life care as a nursing researcher in the psychology of trauma and loss. I became interested in this during my last year in the Army and now focus on the grieving process, particularly related to fathers who have lost children. However, my experience with deathbed visions involves a woman named Dora who was dying from kidney failure.

Dora put up a good fight, but during her last week of life, she started to go in and out of consciousness. The first time it happened, she faded out, but then suddenly seemed lucid and started talking to someone no one else could see. And as time passed, she started looking over or around her family members and me (as if we were in the way) and up at the ceiling more often, carrying on a conversation with her invisible visitor.

When her kidney failure had reached the terminal stage—the critical point—she began talking out loud to her deceased mother. "Mommy?" she asked, as if she were still a child. "Is that you?"

Those of us watching were amazed as Dora continued talking: "Mommy, you're back!" She was clearly seeing her mother as if she were right there in the room. Dora's voice was so genuine and adamant that I often had the urge to turn my head to look for the person she was addressing, even though I knew I wouldn't see anyone there.

At first Dora's daughter, Myra, was upset when she heard her mother talking to her grandmother. But then she became enthralled as she listened to her mom describe a "robe of light" surrounding her mother.

"My goodness!" Dora exclaimed. "Look at the robe you're wearing. It's so bright I can hardly keep my eyes on it. I've never seen anything like this!"

Myra, who didn't see the vision, simply told her mother, "I love you."

That seemed to snap Dora out of her vision, and she looked her directly in the eyes, saying, "Myra, I love you, too." Yet soon afterward, she quickly began talking with her invisible mother again.

It was extremely beautiful to watch and was quite different from what I had ever experienced because the patient herself was completely stunned by the vision. Dora was as amazed and surprised as anyone could be that her deceased mother was in the room with her and draped in robes so spectacular and bright that she had to look away.

At one point while this was going on, I asked Myra what she did for a living.

"I teach special-needs kids in primary school."

"And what did your grandmother do?" I asked, wondering why she was appearing in the midst of so much light.

"She was a housewife, but also spent a lot of her time volunteering at the local hospital," Myra told me.

I'll never forget the day that Dora died. I asked Myra afterward what she thought about the experience, and she told me through tears that it was beautiful for her, not awkward or strange. She felt this way mainly because she could envision her mom being carried over, in a sense, by her own mother.

When I look back, there's no doubt in my mind that Dora was seeing her mother, a kind of guest from the spiritual realms. I'm not a religious guy—I never was—yet the vision didn't seem impossible to me. In fact, it seemed like a natural progression.

Parents usually die before their children, and I see them sort of leading the way when it's the child's turn. It's as if a father dies before his son so that he can come back and show him that death really isn't so bad after all. Our parents are waiting for us on the other side. When I really think about it, I have to admit the idea that our loved ones are watching over us makes perfect sense to me.

Over time, I've seen that visions can be very comforting for patients. And I will always remember Dora and the peace she felt from gazing upon her mother wearing the spectacular, brightly shining robe.

A MOTHER'S VISIT

by Clara

As an ICU nurse, I see it all: car accidents, heart attacks, and trauma like you would not believe. Some stories just stand out in my mind, though. I remember this particular one because it involved a family member.

My niece Jessica, a 26-year-old teacher, taught special education and was visiting our farm for Labor Day weekend. We were all very excited because our family had just purchased a black-and-white spotted horse named Dawn whom the kids loved. The grandkids, nieces, nephews, and the rest of us were gathered together to celebrate the holiday and play with the new horse.

At one point during the party, some of the kids decided to ride Dawn. I wanted everyone to have a good time, but my better judgment told me that this was a risky undertaking, especially since our family had had the horse only a day or two at this point.

Jessica, an expert rider who is also a little bit hardheaded, volunteered to ride Dawn first so I'd relax and feel safe when the others followed her lead. I reminded Jessica that while she was a really good rider, she hadn't ridden for a few months, and the horse had only just arrived. She didn't know Dawn's quirks yet.

Unafraid, Jessica mounted the horse, who was becoming more and more agitated. By the time she gripped the reins, the horse shied and took off. Jessica was thrown and landed in a field, and she was unconscious when we rushed to her. I can distinctly remember hearing one of the kids whisper, "I think she's dead!"

She was still unconscious when the ambulance arrived, but as soon as the paramedics began to work on her, she began to come to. The trouble was, however, that she had no memory of where she was or what had happened. In fact, she couldn't remember anything at all.

When Jessica arrived at the emergency room, she still had no idea who any of us were or that she'd been in an accident. For a few days, her doctor suspected that she was having a brain bleed, and the neurologists confirmed it with an MRI. I sat at Jessica's bedside during that terrible period when you don't know if your loved one is going to make it.

Suddenly, Jessica blurted out, "Mom, it's you! I can't believe you're here!"

Her mother had died in 1995, about six years earlier, and I knew Jessica to be a practical and realistic kind of person. She herself would never have believed in seeing visions of deceased family members. I was shocked and afraid, because after working in hospital ICUs for years and being around so many dying people, I knew that seeing a deceased relative usually meant one thing. So I took Jessica's talking to her mother as a sign of her impending death, almost as certain as her heart stopping.

"Mother! Mother!" Jessica kept calling out. But what she said next really confused me. "Mother? Turn around . . . here I am! Why won't you look at me anymore?"

I was sure that Jessica had seen her mother, but I couldn't understand why she was asking her to turn around. She continued pleading with her mother, saying tearfully, "It's so good to see you, but why won't you face me? Why are you walking away?"

I didn't know what to make of what I was hearing. Some of our family and friends were coming in and out of the room, and I noticed that they were really worried and kind of freaked out. "Why is she talking to her dead mother?" most of them asked. We all watched the tears pouring down Jessica's cheeks as she sobbed, saying, "Mom is gone again."

I will never forget it because it felt so real. Jessica had the saddest look on her face, especially at one point when she said that her mother was walking away. I could even feel the shift in the room because of the intensity of Jessica's emotions when she realized her mother wasn't coming back. I'd never seen my niece cry like this before, but her tears were those of someone who had just been rejected.

"It was so good to see her again," Jessica remarked, still crying. She inhaled deeply and simply stated, "Gone." Then she quickly fell asleep.

The next morning when Jessica woke up, her memory had returned to her, but she didn't remember the vision or the accident. And to this day, she has no memory of falling from the horse, being rushed to the hospital, or having a conversation with her mother.

I was terrified at the time because I thought that seeing her mom meant that my niece was dying, but I learned that that wasn't necessarily the case. Extraordinary things happen; I know that Jessica's mother came to her, and then she turned away and left.

In all of my years at the ICU, I've witnessed my share of deathbed visions and have always known that when a patient experiences them, it means death is imminent. In this particular case, I can only guess that it simply wasn't Jessica's time to go.

• ◇ •

AN ENLIGHTENED PHYSICIAN

by Don

The first time I ever realized that a patient was having a vision involved a family I'd known for many years. (This was back in the days when one general physician would treat everyone in the family and be there for all of the births and deaths.) My patient had survived a radical prostatectomy and had barely regained his bladder control when he came down with hepatitis. He eventually had a blood-transfusion reaction and was in a coma, dying. His wife and son were at his side when he passed.

A decade later, this man's widow, Regina, was dying from heart failure. Once again, I was the attending physician.

She had been close to her family, especially since her husband had died. Now Regina was very sick but had still managed to attend her grandson's graduation from business school. But shortly afterward, it was clear that her condition was quickly deteriorating.

When her children were at her bedside toward the end, she was on a small amount of morphine to dull her pain, but not enough to induce delirium. Regina soon began talking to someone who clearly wasn't there, so her family believed that the medication was causing her to hallucinate. But when they asked me to discontinue the morphine and noticed that she was still carrying on the same conversation, no one could blame it on the drug.

On one occasion, Regina suddenly looked over at her son and said, "I was just with your father."

She went on to speak to her deceased husband for a few minutes, and then came back to carry on a completely coherent conversation with her family. Shortly afterward, she went back into the vision and talked to her husband, eventually "returning" and addressing her son who was sitting by her bedside.

As a physician, I've witnessed some interesting things, especially when I worked in hospice. I've lost count of how many times I've heard a dying patient say, "I saw Jesus," "I saw Moses," or "I saw my husband [or wife, friend, or child]."

People often ask me why doctors don't talk more about visions, and I explain that there are many reasons. First of all, they aren't really there with the patient much at the end of his or her life. They come in for a quick assessment and see how to manage nausea, fatigue, fever, or pain. They're trained to heal and fix, so deathbed visions are considered hallucinations. For more enlightened physicians, however, they might perceive these visions as a sign of impending death. Many of my colleagues would never admit or even discuss such a thing, though, and pass it off as a side effect of medication or lack of oxygen.

When I worked in hospice, I realized that doctors have more time to sit with their patients and get to know them. While there, I was able to witness so many of my patients experiencing visions before dying, and they always seemed to bring peace and reconciliation. I consider these visions to be nothing short of miraculous.

As you can see from these stories, deathbed visions are often a powerful experience for the living as well as the dying.

We will never be able to prove the existence of visions, but we can control how we perceive a person's experience. Does it have value simply because it is authentic and meaningful for the individual? Can the medical community be comfortable with a phenomenon that is outside the realm of explanation? Some interesting questions to pose are these: If a large number of scientists can accept that God is real, can they also have faith and trust the visions of the dying? If not, can traditional Western medicine ever respectfully disagree, or will it continue to discount and minimize something that it doesn't understand? The reality remains the same: as the dying see less of this world, some appear to be looking into the world to come.

After listening to so many doctors and nurses share their stories, I realized that they most often describe their experiences with deathbed visions as profound. They say, "I don't think it was a side effect of a medication, nor was it due to a lack of oxygen . . . it was just a profound moment." They weren't talking about the scientific, technical aspects of dying; they were referring to the art of dying. This made me wonder, How are the dying and deathbed visions portrayed in our cultural expression, particularly in our books and movies?

CHAPTER FOUR

DEATHBED VISIONS
IN THE ARTS

*"It is a far, far better thing that I do, than I have ever done;
it is a far, far better rest that I go to, than I have ever known."*
— final words of Sydney Carton,
from *A Tale of Two Cities* by Charles Dickens

Many people consider the notion of deathbed visions as either some type of New Age spiritualism or a by-product of the contemporary hospice era; however, we need only look to the arts to confirm the prevalence of such phenomena throughout history. The truth is that our novels and films are filled with stories and references of visions.

Some could argue that artists employ deathbed visions in their work solely as literary devices—that is, they're used to push the plot in a certain direction or create a special effect. But they've popped up so often throughout the ages and are so similar in style that their usage goes beyond a "tool" to foreshadow events or evoke an emotional response from the audience.

I'm reminded of the saying "Art imitates life" here—visions exist in our books and movies because they are part of the human experience. They're tucked into our stories to make our uncertainty and fears more bearable—not only because they comfort us, but also because they reflect a truth that's beyond our comprehension.

In this chapter, I'll share just a brief sampling of death-bed visions (along with a few references to "trips" and "crowded rooms") from some of our most popular classic and modern works.

Deathbed Visions in Literature

Readers in mid-19th-century America would have been horrified if Little Eva, from Harriet Beecher Stowe's classic novel *Uncle Tom's Cabin* (1852), had died in agony with no indication that her contribution to the fight against slavery would be rewarded. People all over the world were deeply affected by Stowe's story of the American South and Little Eva's fate—so it would have crushed the hearts of millions to see her abruptly slip into oblivion.

In the scene just prior to the young girl's death, we find the smallest bit of consolation in the form of a vision, slipped into a conversation between Uncle Tom and Miss Feely:

> "Uncle Tom, did Miss Eva say she felt more unwell than usual to-night?"
>
> "No but she told me, this morning, she was coming nearer, — thar's them that tells it to the child, Miss Feely. It's the angels, — 'it's the trumpet sound afore the break o' day,'" said Tom.

This exchange suggests that Eva had an angelic visit. It might not be exactly what we wanted most for her, but it's still comforting to know that she's in heaven. We're grateful that the author didn't abandon her audience or Little Eva.

Visions in literature are referred to by some as "consolation prizes"—that is, they're concocted for the purpose of consoling a grieving loved one or someone who is dying.

Critics only see the concept of "deus ex machina" (an artificial or improbable device that resolves the difficulties of a plot), someone or something arriving in the eleventh hour to save the day . . . or at least affirm our faith and make us feel better about the situation.

The assumption exists that events in a story must be completely resolved so that readers are fulfilled and feel satisfied. When such an expectation appears to be blocked by a character's imminent death, an otherworldly vision may be introduced. This supplies, both for the character and the reader, what acclaimed British critic Frank Kermode has elegantly called "the sense of an ending."

A good example is the contemporary best-selling book *The Lovely Bones* by Alice Sebold, which was written from a visionary perspective. The narrator is a young girl, Susie Salmon, who had been brutally killed. From heaven, Susie is able to observe the life she left behind and comment on the events that follow her death. This technique provides comfort for readers: although her murder was shocking and horrific, we know right from the start that in a certain sense, she's okay. Throughout the story, she is with us, watching her family cope, grow, and live. We're left with an innate feeling that Susie is ever present and will most likely be there to greet her loved ones when they die.

I challenge the notion that visions in literature are simply made up to supply artificial solutions to problems in the plot. In real life, death is more than a "dramatic problem," and deathbed visions appear to be a solution from an unseen world that have provided much comfort—to the dying as well as to those who are grieving.

•◇•

Although deathbed visions are often regarded today as a product of weakness or psychosis, when we look back in time, the oldest storytellers regarded them (and their very close siblings, dreams) as forms of privileged information. In fact, visions date back to the very foundation of the Western literary tradition and belong to every age, including our own.

We can think of visions in literature as the FedEx of the gods, a means by which they communicate with and influence humanity. For instance, a vision might be ominously prophetic, especially when death is lurking around the corner. Take, for example, the *Epic of Gilgamesh* from ancient Mesopotamia, and one of the earliest known literary works. In this epic poem, Enkidu doesn't celebrate when he and his beloved comrade Gilgamesh slay a monster because he had a terrifying dream (in the epic's Book VII) that the gods would "take him away" if he destroyed the monster. Enkidu shares his premonition with Gilgamesh, eerily predicting: "I will sit with the dead in the underworld."

Other visions lack the clarity of Enkidu's; rather, they're filled with symbolism, and it may take some time for their meaning to be revealed. In Sir Thomas Malory's *Le Morte d'Arthur* (1485), prior to his final cataclysmic battle against Mordred, King Arthur has an unsettling vision of his future in which he sees himself dressed "in the richest cloth of gold that might be made." But in that same vision, he also observes himself sitting in a chair above "hideous deep black water, and therein was all manner of serpents."

Although this image sends a clear (and ominous) message to the readers, Arthur isn't certain of his fate. He goes forward with the battle, and in stopping Mordred's forces, is himself mortally wounded. A boat carries him away to Avalon, the mystical realm that hovers between life and death. Arthur is gone, but his legend remains, glowing through the centuries like the rich cloth he wore in the dream.

The veil between the seen and unseen also lifts when we're in dire need of encouragement or help. A good example of this can be seen in *The Goblet of Fire*, the fourth install-ment of the enormously popular Harry Potter series. Near the climactic end of the book, Harry sees the spirits of his parents and friend Cedric, who were killed by the evil Voldemort. Harry's loved ones offer him comfort in a terrifying moment and even help him reach safety. It shouldn't be surprising to find lots of these visions in young-adult fiction, as it mirrors our desire to believe in the afterlife and the notion that death cannot sever the bonds of love.

In Shakespeare's *Henry V,* the beloved character Falstaff dies offstage, alone and miserable, yet there's a suggestion of a vision he experienced, as accounted by Mistress Quickly:

> Nay, sure, he's not in hell: he's in Arthur's bosom, if ever man went to Arthur's bosom. 'A made a finer end, and went away an it had been any christom child; 'a parted ev'n just between twelve and one, ev'n at the turning o' th' tide; for after I saw him fumble with the sheets, and play with flowers, and smile upon his fingers' end, I knew there was but one way; for his nose was as sharp as a pen, and 'a babbl'd of green fields. 'How now, Sir John!' quoth I 'What, man, be o' good cheer.' So 'a cried out 'God, God, God!' three or four times. Now I, to comfort him, bid him 'a should not think of God; I hop'd there was no need to trouble himself with any such thoughts yet. So 'a bade me lay more clothes on his feet; I put my hand into the bed and felt them, and they were as cold as any stone; then I felt to his knees, and so upward and upward, and all was as cold as any stone.

We expect that Falstaff is talking about a final redemptive glimpse of a world beyond, a world that will soon receive him.

Similarly, the character Artemio Cruz in Carlos Fuentes's 1962 masterpiece, *The Death of Artemio Cruz*, recalls the formative moments of his life from his deathbed: "I touch . . . I smell . . . I see . . . I taste . . . I hear . . . they bring me. . . . I pass, touching, smelling, tasting, seeing, smelling the sumptuous carvings."

"Sitting down, catching your breath," Fuentes writes, "you will open to the vast, immediate panorama: the light of the sky crowded with stars will reach you constantly and forever . . . and the winking lights will go on bathing you."

In these final jubilant moments of consciousness, Artemio expresses our deepest wishes about death: that it will be a door opening into something cosmic and transcendent. In this instance, rather than a message from the Divine, the vision conveys a powerful sense of yearning.

I'm also reminded of the gentle character Smike in Charles Dickens's *Nicholas Nickleby* (1839). Smike is an enormously sympathetic figure, and his death is handled delicately by the author:

> He fell into a light slumber, and waking smiled as before; then, spoke of beautiful gardens, which he said stretched out before him, and were filled with figures of men, women, and many children, all with light upon their faces; then, whispered that it was Eden—and so died.

In the modern musical play *Les Miserables*, which is based on the novel by Victor Hugo, a deathbed vision brings the tale full circle. Early on in the story, Fantine died and left her daughter in the loving care of Jean Valjean, pleading to him to give her daughter a better life than she'd had. Valjean honors her request. Years later, when he is dying, Fantine returns to him in a vision and leads him to heaven. In the novel, Valjean's death is expressed in a similar otherworldly manner:

> He had fallen back, the light from the candlesticks fell across him; his white face looked up toward heaven. . . . The night was starless and very dark. Without any doubt, in the gloom, some mighty angel was standing, with outstretched wings, waiting for the soul.

In his 1949 play *Death of a Salesman,* Arthur Miller embodies the deathbed vision in an actual character, Ben Loman, Willy's deceased older brother. Toward the end, Ben convinces Willy that the best way to help his son Biff financially is to embark on an adventure to find diamonds (these are how Ben made his fortune, and they symbolize the tangible wealth that Willy was unable to attain for his family):

> BEN (with promise): It's dark there, but full of diamonds.
> WILLY: Can you imagine that magnificence with twenty thousand dollars in his pocket?
> LINDA (calling from her room): Willy! Come up!
> WILLY (calling into the kitchen): Yes! Yes. Coming! It's very smart, you realize that, don't you, sweetheart? Even Ben sees it. I gotta go, baby. 'By! 'By! (Going over to Ben almost dancing.) Imagine? When the mail comes he'll be ahead of Bernard again!
> BEN: A perfect proposition all around.
> WILLY: Did you see how he cried to me? Oh, if I could kiss him, Ben!
> BEN: Time, William, time!

WILLY: Oh, Ben, I always knew one way or another we were gonna make it, Biff and I!
BEN (looking at his watch): The boat. We'll be late. (He moves slowly off into the darkness.)

The "adventure" is Willy's death; he ultimately decides that the only way he can provide for his family is to kill himself so they can collect his life-insurance policy. The boat in this vision represents the "trip" that Willy believes he must take, sealing his fate.

In *The Leopard* (Giuseppe Tomasi di Lampedusa's 1958 novel about a Sicilian prince), Don Fabrizio likewise experiences a deathbed vision as an impending trip. A melancholic figure out of sync with his wife, his family, and the changing political climate of his country, Fabrizio is comforted by an enigmatic, beautiful visitor who symbolizes an angel of death. The author describes the end of Fabrizio's life as awaiting a train:

> Suddenly amid the group appeared a young woman, slim, in brown traveling dress and wide bustle, with a straw hat trimmed by a speckled veil which could not hide the sly charm of her face. She slid a little suede-gloved hand between one elbow and another of the weeping kneelers, apologized, drew closer. It was she, the creature forever yearned for, coming to fetch him; strange that one so young should yield to him; the time for the train's departure must be very close.

While various media outlets insist that Westerners live in a "postreligious age" and are concerned with death solely as a technical struggle to stay alive, it's clear that not all of our literature reflects that notion. Today, the publishing industry continues to focus on our preoccupation with understanding life's final moments and what may or may not wait beyond them. Although some novelists eschew anything suggestive of fantasy, not all fiction writers are so restrained. Some concentrate on our fascination with immortality, reassuring us that an afterlife exists or that life itself doesn't necessarily come to an end for some. Examples include the extremely popular and best-selling *Twilight* series by Stephenie Meyer as well as the vampire books of her predecessor Anne Rice.

Some contemporary novelists haven't retreated from the deathbed vision of Dickens or Stowe, either. There's Isabel Allende, for instance. In her 1982 novel, *The House of the Spirits,* the author imagines the protagonist's grandmother coming to keep her dying grandfather company in his last days:

> She did not leave him for a second, following him around the house, peering over his shoulder when he was reading in his library, lying down beside him and leaning her beautiful curly head against his shoulder when he got into bed. At first she was just a mysterious glow, but as my grandfather slowly lost the rage that had tormented him throughout his life, she appeared as she had been at her best, laughing with all her teeth and stirring up the other spirits as she sailed through the house.

Deathbed Visions in Films

Movies are also doing their part to reflect the phenomenon of deathbed visions. Death is often a central theme in many story lines on the big screen; in fact, visions and spirits of the deceased visiting their loved ones is a common occurrence.

Take a moment to think about it and I bet you can name several films that include deathbed visions, spirits crowding the rooms of the living, and references to going home.

In Steven Spielberg's *Saving Private Ryan,* audiences were shown the devastating costs of war in a way cinema had never presented before. In a pivotal scene, the company's only field medic, Irwin Wade (Giovanni Ribisi), is mortally wounded in an unplanned raid. As he lay dying while his comrades try to stanch the bleeding, his final words are a cry to his mother and the assertion that he's going home.

As I've mentioned previously, the most common death-bed vision includes a visit from one's mother, and the notion of going home is so often uttered by the dying. There's no screenwriting class or book that will tell you to always use someone's mother for a deathbed vision or to get everyone "home" in the end. So why does this happen so frequently? Are these writers just reflecting upon real experiences, or does this hit some primal chord that exists deep within us all?

In *Terms of Endearment,* we laughed and then cried, especially when Emma Horton (played by Debra Winger) dies in the end. Only the consolation that Garrett Breedlove (Jack Nicholson) offers Emma's mother, Aurora Greenway (Shirley MacLaine), keeps us going. (By that time, we've also become hooked on the dying Emma's relationship with her mother.) Not to be left there, we were eventually taken back home to Texas in the sequel, *The Evening Star.* When Aurora is dying, who comes to comfort her? Her deceased daughter, Emma, of course.

The notion of a crowd of spirits surrounding the dying person also has its share of roles. Let's think back to the blockbuster *Titanic.* Although Jack (Leonardo DiCaprio's character) succumbs to hypothermia hours after the ship sinks, we see that Rose (Kate Winslet) survives and goes on to live a full life. Story over? Not really. What do the moviemakers do? At the very end, Rose (by now an old woman) is lying in bed, and we're swept back to the RMS *Titanic* in all its glory. The audience is unsure if she is dreaming or has died in her sleep, but there we see young Rose reuniting with Jack on the grand staircase as a crowd of passengers cheer and applaud.

To simply show the two lovers reunited would have disregarded everyone else on the ship. What if death is that way, too? That is, what if there are crowds of people who greet the dying . . . much more often than we realize? A good example is in the movie *Ghost*. When Sam (played by Patrick Swayze) is at peace and his spirit can finally depart, he doesn't just walk off into the light; a crowd is waiting for him.

Even in our comedies—from *Ghost Town* to *Beetlejuice*—people never seem to be alone in death. In *Thelma & Louise,* played brilliantly by Geena Davis and Susan Sarandon, we witness the women soaring to their deaths after driving a 1960s Ford Thunderbird convertible into the Grand Canyon. When the credits roll, we then see the actors alive again. We know that they're just earlier scenes from their lives, and they're there to help us focus on how they lived rather than on the violence of their deaths. Yet when we look deeper, I believe that this technique plays to our primal desire to transcend death.

In the film version of *Wuthering Heights,* based on the classic novel by Emily Brontë, the two lovers are finally together again in death. Heathcliff (played by Laurence Olivier) carries a dying Cathy (Merle Oberon) in his arms to her bedroom window, where they look out on the moors and Peniston Crag where they played together as children. Before her last breath, they make a promise to be together for eternity. And in the film's final image, their ghosts are seen walking up to the Crag.

Science fiction deals with visions and immortality as well. At the end of *Star Wars Episode VI: Return of the Jedi,* for example, we're at the celebration of the destruction of the Death Star; but all those who had died are not forgotten, as Luke Skywalker gazes upon the smiling faces of Obi-Wan Kenobi, Yoda, and Anakin . . . and waves good-bye.

It wasn't a surprise for me to find deathbed visions in the arts. In fact, I would have been concerned if I hadn't found references and archetypes illuminating whom and what we see before we die. I believe that we'll continue to watch and read about the visions that comfort the dying because that is what resonates in our souls. What a wonderful experience to be greeted by our loved ones, who take us on the final journey to our heavenly home. The arts will always reflect this truth because, just as Dorothy affirms: "There's no place like home."

Let's return to more firsthand accounts of deathbed visions—these are stories told by professionals from the mental-health perspective.

CHAPTER FIVE

VISIONS OF
THE DYING

Part II

"Now I want to go home."
— final words of Vincent van Gogh

These next stories come from professional counselors with formal training and licensure. They are often the ones who help the dying manage the emotional upheaval that comes with saying good-bye to all that they've known. Those who are in the mental-health arena are often keenly aware of what is or isn't authentic. They spend their lives feeling the emotions of others and know how to tell the difference between a patient with confusion or hallucinations and one who has an extraordinary experience, such as a deathbed vision. A book of this nature wouldn't be complete without hearing their stories firsthand.

•◇•

No Tip Required

by Angela

I am a psychologist who works with families and couples, and I specialize in addiction and chemical dependencies. When I counsel couples with so many problems, I often think back on my own parents, Helen and Milton. It makes me realize what a unique and wonderful relationship they had.

My parents were married for 62 years and could finish each other's sentences. They shared everything, and one of their enduring qualities was a quirky sense of humor. Mom told me that when she found out she was pregnant with me, she'd asked Dad, "You sure *you* don't want to carry this baby?" And when my father got a speeding ticket, the police officer was still standing there when Dad looked over to my mom sitting beside him and said, "Honey, you speed, too. Would you like a ticket?"

My father's sense of humor also carried over to his work as a dentist, and his patients loved having a doctor who could make them laugh. *I* loved laughing with both of my parents, too, and decided they were the funniest parents a girl could have.

My parents used humor for life's serious moments as well. For example, when my mother was diagnosed with breast cancer and needed a radical mastectomy, she quipped, "Oh, Milton, be a man—volunteer *your* breast. You don't need yours like I need mine."

One morning when Mom was getting up, she had a sudden aortic rupture and died instantly. She was 80. Dad did his best to cope, but he'd miss his beloved partner for the rest of his life. He never made those jokes with anyone else, since that form of communication was an integral part of their relationship.

Five years later, my dad was in a hospice unit after a long battle with bladder cancer that had spread throughout his body. My father and I had become especially close after my mom died, and I stayed by his side as much as possible.

Dad was feeling well and reading the Sunday paper one day when I said, "Hey, you're looking a little rough around the edges. How about a shave?"

"Sure," he replied.

Since he was having trouble holding a newspaper, holding a razor would be even more difficult, so I quickly blurted out, "Welcome to Angela's Barbershop!" and started looking around the bathroom. "Dad, did you bring your razor?" I asked.

He couldn't remember, so I called the nurse and asked if she had a spare shaving kit. I walked over to the nurses' station and waited as she gathered the supplies for me. I suddenly heard my dad talking to someone and realized that the nurse hadn't turned off the intercom in his room. I couldn't make out what he was saying but figured that one of his friends must have dropped by. The nurse walked back with me, and we found my father in the room all alone.

"Who were you just talking to, Dad?"

"Helen," he casually replied.

"Helen, as in Mom . . . who is dead?"

"That's the one."

"Do you know that she's dead?" I asked as gently as possible.

"Of course. I was with her when she died."

"And she's here now?"

"Yes. I know it's strange, but it's true."

Here, the nurse chimed in: "It isn't unusual for a dying person to have loved ones come to greet them."

"I've heard that," Dad said, "but I don't believe in it."

"But you just said Mom was here," I reminded him.

"Well, I must be hallucinating from the drugs."

"The only medication you're on is to help with your nausea," the nurse told him, "and it isn't known to impair a person's thinking."

Dad seemed a bit irritated. "Okay, so maybe I'm wrong—maybe we do get visits. Am I going to get a shave or what?"

I gently patted some shaving cream on my father's face. He glanced back to look over his left shoulder and said, "Helen, are you sure you don't want a shave, too?"

When I just stared blankly at him, he explained, "Your mom is laughing."

"What is it, honey?" he asked, as he could see that I was starting to tear up.

"I just realized how much I've missed listening to you and Mom joke around." During the rest of the time, he continued talking to my mother. After he'd been quiet for a while, I asked if she was still in the room.

"I see her but still don't quite believe it. Maybe I really am hallucinating."

I said, "I work all day with people who hallucinate because they're hooked on opiates and pain meds, but you're not on either of those, and this doesn't seem like a hallucination. I know you so well, and this is exactly how it felt when you and Mom were together. I just wish I could see her, too."

He looked in the direction where my mother was. "Can Angela see you?" he suddenly asked. It seemed as if he were interpreting a foreign language when he finally replied, "She loves you very much, but it's not time for you to see her."

"Is she, um, solid looking, or does she look like a ghost?"

"She's a solid figure . . . and a nice figure at that. No ghost here!" he assured me. "You know, when I was a kid, I learned that the smallest thing in the entire world was an atom. End of story. That was the fact, but now we know that there's so much more . . . so maybe your mom really is here."

"How do you feel right now?" I asked, always the therapist.

"Happy! I'm with my wife of more than 60 years." He paused for a moment and then went on. "You know how much I love you, Angela. If your mom can be here for me, then we'll *both* come for you when it's time. But for now, I think I'd like to take a nap with my clean-shaven face."

"That sounds fine, and by the way, no tip required. You go spend some time with Mom. I love you."

"I love you, too," he said, closing his eyes. Almost as if he were in a dream, his lips mouthed some words as he dropped off to sleep for the night.

Dad died the next day. I now know that love is more powerful than I ever thought possible, because not even death could diminish the bond between my parents.

An Unexpected Visitor

by Diane

I am a counselor, and at the "young" age of 60, I learned that deathbed visions are real. The experience taught me that who we meet might be totally different from whom we *expect* to meet.

My birth father died when I was six years old, and I was raised by my wonderful stepfather, Jim. He married my mother when I was ten; and my sister, two brothers, and I took to him instantly. Jim had seven siblings, so we also got five new uncles and two aunts in the deal.

Jim stepped into his role as father naturally, being there at my high-school graduation and walking me down the aisle when I got married. He and his family lovingly filled a part of my world that had been missing ever since my birth father died.

Decades later, I'm finally ready to talk about a subject that's important to many of the clients I counsel. Of course I didn't think about it at the time, but I never realized that all those uncles and aunts who brought so much life and joy to my family would also bring death and heartache. I watched over the years as Jim lost sibling after sibling.

As my dear stepdad stayed by Hugh's side when he was dying (Hugh was his eldest brother), we were all comforted to learn that Hugh had seen his deceased mother shortly before he died. Well, not all the family members believed that she had visited him. Paul, another brother, thought it was baloney, saying that Hugh was probably just thinking about her at the time.

However, days before another uncle passed away, once again our grandmother made a visit. Paul, the doubting uncle, still insisted that the visions were a result of "just missing your mom when you're dying."

As my remaining aunts and uncles passed away over the years, I couldn't help but wonder if they were forming their own greeting party in the afterlife. Then I got word one day that my uncle Paul had died suddenly of a heart attack. At the funeral, I was curious to learn if our grandmother had come to him, despite all of his doubts. No one would ever know, unfortunately, since he died alone.

Sometime later, I got an urgent call from my mom that Jim was in the hospital, and he was doing poorly. I flew home immediately, hoping for the best but knowing that health and age weren't on his side. He'd been fighting chronic heart failure for many years.

My stepfather was released from the hospital, but he was so frail that he seemed to be practically melting into the bed. He was surrounded by his wife and four children, all of us grown up. We knew his steady decline was irreversible, but despite how weak he felt, Jim still managed to get out a joke or two to lighten the mood and would call every home-care nurse who came by his "favorite."

Over the next few days, however, I watched Jim's body grow weaker. He spoke less often, and stories became paragraphs and paragraphs became sentences. I thought about his siblings who'd died over the years: Would they all come to meet him? Would there be a family reunion? How about my doubting Uncle Paul, who never believed in visions? Would he be there?

As my stepdad's last days were upon him, I stopped thinking about it, mainly because I was so focused on helping my mom. One day, though, one of my parents' friends was visiting, and she and my mother were chatting in the kitchen. I was with Jim when he suddenly looked up and asked, "Who are you?" Then he began a conversation that only he could understand. I just listened as he talked: "I was honored to be there, and I'm so glad you saw it all. You're welcome—I'm grateful to you, too."

My thoughts were racing: *Could he really be having a vision? Was his mom here, or maybe one of his siblings? Was it Uncle Paul, the skeptic? Or perhaps Hugh, the oldest brother who had died first?* I couldn't contain myself any longer and asked, "Dad, who are you talking to?"

"Buddy. It's Buddy."

"Who's that?"

"He was thanking me for being a good dad."

I was confused. All of my siblings were still living. Did Jim have a child I didn't know about who had died? Since he didn't say anything else, I left the room and went to the kitchen where my mom was. "Do you know someone named Buddy?" I asked her.

"My goodness, I hadn't thought of that name in years," she replied. "Where did you hear that?"

"Dad just said it."

"Jim used to tease your father when they were in high school," Mom said. "As a joke, he'd call him Buddy, as if he didn't remember his name."

"Dad knew my biological father?"

"Yes. They weren't that close and didn't hang out. I was the only person they had in common."

Suddenly, I realized what had just happened. My birth father had come to greet the man who had raised my siblings and me. He wanted to *thank* Jim for taking care of his children since he couldn't.

"Mom, my dad was just here! He was talking to Jim and thanking him for being such a great father."

Mom and I cried together and were so grateful for my birth father's visit and his message of love.

An Old Language

by Keith

I've been a social worker in hospice services since 1983. I originally worked as a psychiatric technician to help pay my way through school, but I never realized how much that training would later help in my career.

I remember my first job working in an adolescent facility. Basically, it was for those who couldn't make it at home. The staff of psychiatrists and psychologists would meet with the teens daily, but the techs like me worked in the dorms day in and day out.

After I earned my master's degree, I found out that a professional organization was looking for recent grads who wanted to work in hospice, and I decided I was up for the challenge. So, in an interesting turn of events, I went from caring for lively, rambunctious teens to those preparing for death.

Although I never imagined ending up in hospice, it turned out to be the best place I've ever worked. Every day, I've seen and learned new things.

I remember one particular patient, a woman named Maria, who was in her late 80s. She was dying of metastatic breast cancer and had been unresponsive for the last 24 hours; in fact, she hadn't said a word at all during the previous week. But suddenly, she became alert and began speaking in Czech as she pointed at several objects in her room.

Maria's two daughters were amazed because they hadn't heard their mother speak in her native language for many years. Since they couldn't understand it, they called one of their aunts to come over and interpret. They were concerned that their mother might be in pain or was trying to tell them something important before she died.

Finally, Aunt Anna arrived, a little frail herself, and sat down to hear what her older sister was saying. A strange look came over her face as she explained, "Maria is talking to people in our family who have already died. But it's more than just talking—she can see them."

"Is that why she keeps pointing and looking in the corner of the room? Does she know who she's seeing?" one daughter asked. "I'm not so sure about this. Maybe Mom is hallucinating or having some type of psychiatric issue caused by a medication."

"I used to work in a psychiatric unit for adolescents," I told the family. "I don't believe that Maria is hallucinating or experiencing any mental issues. She looks very peaceful."

Anna, who was still listening to her sister talking, said, "It's our mother and grandparents. She's really happy to see them again. And she's speaking Czech because they don't know any English."

It was amazing to watch this once unresponsive woman suddenly become animated and lively. It was also heartwarming to know how happy and relieved Maria's daughters were.

When I started in hospice, I was skeptical of deathbed visions and anything that referred to the afterlife. But the more I've heard about these stories—and have even been in the room with many of my own patients as they were visited by deceased loved ones—it makes me question my own spirituality and religious upbringing. Accepting the truth has been a growth experience. The fact that visions bring comfort to so many reminds me that not everything can be seen or logically explained.

◆

YOU DID WHAT?!

by Ellen

As a counselor in private practice, I've had many encounters with terminal illnesses and death. Yet despite all of that experience, I still wasn't prepared when I lost my sister, Mary Beth. My parents had both died when I was in my 20s, so my family consisted of my sister, my brother, and myself. When Mary Beth was diagnosed with pancreatic cancer, it was an especially tough blow.

During her final weeks in the hospital, my brother, Larry, and I were taking turns so that our sister was never alone. I was trying to be realistic about the grim situation, but Larry kept hoping she'd beat the cancer.

One night when I was alone with Mary Beth, she was in terrible pain. "Are you okay?" I asked her. "What do you need?"

She groaned. I leaned in and gently said, "What are you trying to say?"

"I want to go now," she mumbled. "Mom and Dad are calling me . . . they want me to go with them."

I didn't understand what she meant. I just couldn't comprehend it at first. I thought that she must be in a lot of pain and felt so sorry for what she was enduring. All I wanted to do was try to give her a bit of relief, so I called the nurse and asked her to give my sister some pain medication.

"Do you really want to go to Mom and Dad?" I asked.

"Yes," she replied quietly, reaching her hands up toward the ceiling.

I started to cry and said, "Please don't leave me. I love you so much."

"Let me go, Ellen," Mary Beth pleaded. "Mom and Dad are here for me."

While we waited for the nurse to administer the drugs, I silently acknowledged that my sister was seeking a more permanent kind of relief. I thought about calling Larry (he'd left the hospital a few hours earlier) to let him know that Mary Beth was seeing our dead parents, but I decided to let him get a good night's sleep and call him first thing in the morning.

My sister continued to repeat that our parents were waiting for her. Without a great deal of forethought, I told her, "I love you, and if you want to go with Mom and Dad, you can."

The nurse arrived and gave Mary Beth some pain medication, and she and I both fell asleep. When I woke up in the morning and called my brother to tell him what had happened, he drove right over to the hospital. By the time he got there, though, our sister had taken a turn for the worse and was in an unresponsive state. Larry said her name a few times and gently shook her. "What happened?" he demanded.

"I don't know," I answered. "I just told her that if she needed to go, it was okay."

"You did what?!" Larry was irate. "How could you do that? If she dies, I'll never forgive you for telling her it was okay to go!" Even after I told him that Mary Beth kept pleading with me to let her go with our parents, he still remained furious with me.

My sister died later that day, and Larry became fixated on what I'd said to her. He also completely dismissed the idea that our parents may have come to her bedside to bring her home.

I derive some comfort from the fact that my parents came to greet Mary Beth. She certainly wasn't scared at the end; their presence brought her much peace. I also didn't feel like I was encouraging my sister to give up or that I had the power to prevent her death—I was simply acknowledging her experience and supporting her in whatever way I could.

The vision of our parents coming to my sister made it sacred and profound for me, but unfortunately, my brother didn't see it that way. To this day, he believes that because I gave her permission "to go," I'm partly responsible for her death. I sometimes wonder what would have happened if I'd asked her to stay. I'll never know, but I do know that I followed my instincts. And I really hope that when it's my time, my mother and father will come for me, too.

Fear Doesn't Stop Death—It Stops Life

by Jane

I remember an incident that happened when I was in my sophomore year of premed studies. I'd always been interested in healing because my mother had died years earlier, and I'd been exposed to many physicians and hospital settings. Yet while I knew I wanted to be a doctor, I was often overcome by fear and doubt about whether or not I could make it through the years of school.

I was devastated when I got the news that my father had been diagnosed with gastric cancer. Although I was focused on my studies, I decided to take a leave of absence to help him fight the disease. As I stepped onto the cancer roller coaster, I was committed to facing the difficult challenges that were ahead and quickly learned that it wasn't only an emotional drain, but also a financial one, since there were many necessary treatments that our health insurance didn't cover.

Before all this happened, I'd been getting ready for the MCAT, the Medical College Admission Test, and was overcome with fear and anxiety. I knew this one exam could make or break my career in medicine. But as my father's condition grew worse, I realized that my plan to take off a semester wasn't realistic. This was going to be a much worse ordeal than I had imagined.

I realized that I had to face the fact that the cancer had spread and my dad was dying. It turned out that I was as terrified of losing him as he was of dying. My father had always been a fearful person, but my mother had known how to quell his fears. I'd taken over that role long ago, but Dad and I only had each other. I couldn't imagine my life without him.

Late one night when I'd fallen asleep on the couch next to my father's bed, I woke up hearing his voice. I looked over and saw him reaching toward the ceiling.

"Dad? What's going on? What are you reaching for?"

"She's here."

"Who?"

"Your mother . . . she's right here."

I was in awe. Could it be true? Was it possible that she was actually in the room? "Dad," I said, "what's Mom saying? Tell her how much I miss her."

My father was mesmerized by whatever he was gazing upon, but then started speaking: "She wants us to know that there's nothing to fear. There was never anything to fear. She's been watching over us, and she loves how you've been taking care of me. Now she'll be watching over you and your family. There is nothing to be afraid of."

I wondered what "family" my mother was talking about. After all, I was single and my dad was dying. When he died the next day, I took little comfort in the words he'd said. Both of my parents were now gone, and I felt utterly alone. To make things worse, my savings were diminished, and I had no hope of paying for medical school.

I transferred to a local college and went on to earn my degree in psychology. I became a counselor with a private practice . . . and I met the man I would marry. Within a few years, I had a wonderful husband and two healthy children. I knew this was the family that my mother said she'd be watching over.

Today, nearly 17 years after my father's death, my kids are teenagers, and I'm still inspired by my dad's vision. I recall my mother's words: there is nothing to fear, and there never was. I now realize that fear doesn't stop death—it stops life.

After I was ultimately able to overcome my own fears and doubts, I went back to school to prepare for the MCAT, the test I had begun to study for so many years ago. I now see that while my father's illness temporarily stopped me from going after my dreams, his vision of my mother's encouragement brought my dreams back to life.

PLEASE SHUT THE WINDOWS

by Maggie

I am a counselor in an inpatient hospice unit in Florida. I remember a tragic, challenging, and touching experience I had as a social worker in the late 1980s. My patient's name was Sammy, and he was one of the first people I worked with who had AIDS. The disease was still relatively unknown during that time, so when someone with AIDS checked into the hospital, there was a lot of hysteria and fear among the health-care employees assigned to the infectious-diseases unit.

The nurses were afraid to handle anything that an AIDS patient had touched, and they always wore full gowns when they entered his or her room. Sammy's condition was advanced, and I went to the fourth floor of the hospital to talk with him. I still recall the large room called the "skilled-care unit" that had been empty and was now being used for AIDS patients. The room was rather barren, kind of a sad place with a single vase and table. A colorful personality, Sammy loved to tell stories but never had any visitors, and we had no clue about his former life. He was there with us because he had nowhere else to go and no one to care for him.

Over the next few weeks, I watched Sammy's condition worsen. His hair was going gray, and although he was tall and had broad shoulders, he looked utterly wasted and wrapped the blanket around himself tighter and tighter. He wasn't really eating much, so we asked about his favorite foods. He told us that he liked turnip greens and fried chicken, so we got them for him as a special treat. There was little we could do, and it made us feel less helpless.

Sammy's health went downhill fast, and he started drifting in and out of consciousness. He'd enter a dreamlike state and mutter something in my direction, but it felt like he was talking to someone else. For example, he'd say, "Please shut the windows. Shut the windows."

"The windows are closed," I would tell him, wondering if he felt cold. Then when he would announce, "I'm not ready," I would realize he was talking about death.

One day when he asked me to close the door to his room, I was surprised because he tended to want it open. It really seemed like he was trying to keep himself there in the room, and then he drifted off to sleep.

When I sat with him, I liked to sing lullabies and songs. Now as I hummed a tune, Sammy reached out and touched my hand. Suddenly, he was talking to his mother, reaching his arms out like a baby waiting to be picked up. I listened as he started singing like a small child.

Several times that night, he told me it was very windy and asked me to shut the windows. I went along with it, telling him that he was safe and we were all there if he needed anything. He described the sensation of being lifted off the bed by the wind. Each time he felt the force of the "wind," he asked me to close the windows so he wouldn't be carried away by it. He also started talking to his mother again, which made him much less fearful. At this point, I knew he was seeing a dimension that I simply couldn't share with him. This was new for me. Although I'd seen many people die in the course of my work, this was the first time that I was the only other person in the room.

Eventually I asked Sammy what he was reaching out for earlier.

"I wanted a hug," he replied.

I realized that he probably hadn't been hugged for quite some time, especially since he had AIDS and people were afraid to touch him. Tuning in to my motherly instincts,

I pushed past my own fears and got beside him on his bed and gathered him in my arms. He nestled in, swaying as if he were singing. I sang him a lullaby, which seemed to comfort him. He relaxed in my embrace yet still reached outward. Then he opened his mouth wide and said, "She's here! Mom, you're here!"

As a result of complications of the disease, I knew that Sammy was practically blind, but then I realized that he didn't need eyes for what he was seeing. Reaching out even more, he leaned out of my hug to where he was looking and said again, "Mom, you're here for me." He smiled and drifted into sleep.

When I noticed a respiratory change, I alerted the nurses, who were just happy that someone was dealing with Sammy. I was no longer the least bit fearful, and I held on to him as I felt him drifting away. His breathing rate continued to slow, and he was having difficulty taking breaths. By this time, he'd stopped talking—it felt to me like he was going with "the wind" instead of resisting it.

Sammy was no longer in my embrace but reaching upward, so I gently released my hold on him, offering him back to his own mother. He then collapsed back onto the bed and died. I'd never seen anything like it. He had wanted so much for his mother to hug him, and he got his wish.

May you rest in peace, Sammy.

◆

Not a Ghostly Experience

by Nora

I am a clinical social worker and the director of professional education at an assistance program for cancer survivors. I've been a social worker for 14 years at an outpatient transplant center, and before that, I worked in a hospital oncology unit.

A young man named Eric was one of my patients when I was doing family support. He'd been diagnosed with Hodgkin's lymphoma when he was in college, but after treatment it had gone into remission. Unfortunately, it eventually returned and he required a bone-marrow transplant. He'd recently gotten married; and he and his wife, who were both artists and worked at the local university, came to see one of our top lymphoma specialists. That's how I was introduced to him.

I supported Eric as he and his family went through the emotional drain of cancer, but the disease came back once again even after the transplant. When this occurred, he decided that it was time to seek hospice care when an infection forced him to check into the hospital.

Knowing that Eric was near the end of his life, he and I spent a lot of time talking about his grief. We also discussed his sadness over the things he wasn't going to experience in life. Eric confided that he was distraught that he'd never own a little house with a backyard, have children, or even do simple things like take the garbage out to the curb. He talked about how his grandmother had raised him because his mother had run off when he was young. Nana, however, had died about four or five years previously, and he said that he'd prayed a lot when she was dying but hadn't done so since.

Eric remained in the hospital and was eventually transferred to another unit. At some point, his doctor paged me and informed me that the young man was in the dying process. I went to Eric's room with the chaplain, and we watched him going in and out of consciousness. This was only the third person I'd ever watched die; and I heard him gasping for breath, making what some refer to as the death rattle. The strange thing was that throughout all this, I realized he was talking to his deceased grandmother.

"Nana," he said, in a childlike voice. "I'm here. I'm coming."

Then he seemed to shift from his childhood to the present time, asking, "Nana, do you know that I'm dying? Are you really here?"

I told Eric that I was glad his grandmother was there. He didn't respond but became fixed on a point on the wall to my left, and inquired, "Is that why you came back after all this time?"

I'd never experienced this before. Turning to the doctor, I explained who Eric's grandmother was and that she had died years ago. I added, "Isn't this amazing? What do you think about it?"

The doctor insisted that Eric's brain was losing oxygen and he was probably hallucinating. I went over to him and put my hand on his, which felt cold since his body was shutting down. His last words were: "Nana, I'm coming." I leaned over and whispered, "Your Nana is here for you now." I hope he took some comfort in that.

When I think about the experience, I believe that Eric's grandmother was really there. He was talking to her in the same manner that he'd spoken to me many times before, just as if she were sitting right beside him. It was absolutely authentic. I know that no one can prove whether or not it was real, but it sure felt that way.

Since then, I've tried to be present with my patients when they're dying and do what I can to ensure that they're comfortable and at peace. I'm not a very spiritual person, but I felt a presence in Eric's case and in many others' as well. Not a ghostly experience, but a feeling of holiness . . . as if someone or something is guiding my patients home.

Perfect Timing

by Peter

I got my bachelor's degree in psychology and went on to get my master's in social work. I now work as a therapist. My most memorable story involving a deathbed vision came around the time my dad had a stroke. When he got back from the hospital, my mother was extremely dedicated, and cared for him night and day, but she ran into some problems along the way.

Dad slept on a special bed pad that was designed to eliminate bedsores, so he was staying in the guest room. But he sometimes woke up in the middle of the night and forgot where he was and would try to make his way back to his bedroom. He'd fallen twice in the process. During that second fall, Mom had slept right through it and woke up to him crawling on the floor. Startled, she at first thought a stranger was in the room.

"How could you mistake your own husband for a stranger?" I asked.

"It wasn't like your father had brushed his teeth and was coming to bed," she explained. "He had grabbed my leg, and it wasn't the gentle touch of a husband. I'm not sure which scares me more: the idea of your father falling or a strange man trying to crawl into my bed in the middle of the night."

My brothers and I decided to hire a nurse so that our mother could relax and get some uninterrupted sleep. We thought that would take care of everything, and it did for a while.

One night Mom suddenly woke up, not because of Dad, but because she was having trouble breathing. She was rushed to the hospital and eventually diagnosed with a serious case of COPD (chronic obstructive pulmonary disease).

As a family, we buckled in for a long ride with two parents in poor health. The following day, the phone rang at about 2 A.M. It was the nurse on the unit, informing me that my mom had a code blue and didn't survive. I called my brothers, and we headed to the hospital. We considered waking up Dad and taking him with us, but it was so late and we were afraid it would be too much for him . . . plus, Mom was already gone.

At the hospital, we took care of all the paperwork and were glad that we hadn't woken up our father; at the same time, we also knew we couldn't just wake him up in the morning and act like nothing had happened. I told my brothers that I'd stay at our parents' house and tell Dad in the morning. But when we pulled up to the house, we were stunned to find all the lights on and wondered what was going on.

We found out soon enough when the nursing assistant answered the door and she was clearly upset. "Your father is going crazy!" she exclaimed. "He woke up screaming that a woman was trying to get into his bed. He said that she had grabbed his leg and was pushing at him. I tried to explain that no one was there, but he insisted that a strange woman *was* there. Then he told me that she was dead! I fell to my knees and started to pray."

"Was he panicked?" I asked her.

"No, but I was," she admitted. "At first, he was surprised that she was there, and then he was angry that she was gone. He was just sitting up in bed, crying."

"What time did this happen?"

"It was almost 2."

"That was when my mother's heart stopped! They tried to resuscitate her but couldn't."

I hate to admit that just as I'd judged my mother for not recognizing my father in the middle of the night, I also judged my father for not recognizing his own wife who had died and was trying to say good-bye. In my mind, after having been married for all those years, his final *coup de grâce* was that he failed to recognize his own wife at the end of her life. I was angry that he'd just seen her as some random person.

Later, I realized that I was mostly upset because my mother had died alone. I felt sad and guilty about it, imagining that she hadn't wanted to be alone. Wasn't that why she was desperately trying to connect with her husband at the end of her life?

Over time, I came to realize that Mom had tried to reach out and connect with Dad the same way he'd been so desperate to climb in bed and reconnect with her. That was what they both wanted: to be together and never leave each other in body or spirit. It really had nothing to do with me.

My father died one week later to the day. In fact, he made no indication at her funeral that she was gone at all. It was as if he knew she was waiting for him—and I really believe she was.

•◇•

I MISSED SOMETHING

by Joanne

I'm a social worker with a hospice agency, and when I was a bereavement coordinator, I received a phone call from a woman named Bonnie. She said that she feared she'd done something wrong. Her mother, Elisa, was on our hospice-care service for about six to eight months. As her health deteriorated, she was unable to talk much, so she said very little to her daughter.

As she got closer to death, however, Elisa began to speak about her husband who had died 20 years earlier, saying, "He's coming to visit." She pointed up over the bed and called out, "Arthur!"

Upset about hearing her mother talk to her dead father, Bonnie told her, "Mom, you know that Dad died years ago." She felt that it was important for Elisa to acknowledge the fact that her husband was gone. In essence, her daughter was trying to make her "snap out of it."

"This happens quite a lot," I explained to Bonnie. "People often call out names of loved ones who are already deceased."

"Right." Bonnie seemed irritated. "Seeing dead people is normal."

I backed off, unwilling to argue with someone who was losing her mom. A few months later, after Elisa had passed away, Bonnie called me out of the blue. "I missed something," she said. "My mother was trying to tell me about something that was happening, and I wasn't able to see it."

I gently explained (as if I'd never mentioned it before) that her experience wasn't unusual. "Sometimes we're so focused on taking care of our loved ones—making sure they're comfortable and have whatever they need—we can miss things along the way. Your mother wasn't in distress; in fact, she was talking more at the end, which she hadn't been doing."

Bonnie continued to feel upset and started to cry. "I feel so guilty, like we should have talked about it," she confessed. "I just thought Mom was disoriented, and I really believed that the best thing to do was tell her what was real and what wasn't. I never considered the possibility that what she was experiencing *was* real."

I felt for Bonnie. This isn't the first time I'd counseled family members who thought they'd missed a sign and were left with great regret. As a social worker, I think we could do more to prepare our patients and their family members. We need to talk openly about deathbed visions. We already advise people on so many other issues, such as how to deal with shortness of breath as well as managing pain levels with medication. We discuss the emotional aspects of leaving others behind, saying things like, "It's okay to let go and say good-bye when your loved one's life is over." We share all these details, yet we rarely say, "A deceased loved one might come to greet you." We never tell our patients that there's a difference between near-death awareness and a near-death experience. We don't normalize these occurrences so that people are prepared.

Elisa never came out of focusing on her deceased husband. I can't help but wonder what more I could have done to prepare her family for bereavement. Often, the attending social worker for a dying person ends up facilitating a bereavement group for the loved ones, and I've thought long and hard about how to help Bonnie with the pain of missing her mother as well as her regret over not acknowledging what Elisa was seeing.

I suggested to Bonnie that while she missed the visitation, she had completely been there for her mother. And even more important, Elisa didn't miss her husband's visit. After all, in the end, such experiences are really more for the dying person.

In the world of end-of-life care, we'll never know all the answers or see all the mysteries of death revealed, but we'll each figure it out for ourselves as we go along.

In the earlier chapter titled "Part I," the many accounts of deathbed visions and the dying process were told by doctors and nurses; and in this section, I shared stories from mental-health professionals. As you've seen, their experiences are very similar. I invite you to do your own exploration: the next time you're with doctors or other health-care providers who work with the dying, ask these individuals if they have a story to share. Chances are, they will.

CHAPTER SIX

THE SPIRITUAL AND RELIGIOUS VISIONS

"Jesus, I love you. Jesus, I love you."
— final words of Mother Teresa

In this chapter, we'll look at many examples of spiritually themed visions. After all, we certainly can't talk about death and dying without wondering how God or some other higher power fits in.

Interestingly, I've never come across anyone who experienced a vision outside of his or her own faith—in other words, a Jewish person doesn't see Jesus, and a Christian doesn't see Allah. However, the belief in angels seems to transcend most religious boundaries, and many believe that these ethereal beings play a prominent role in the dying process. We pray that angels will gently guide our loved ones to heaven or be there to greet them when they arrive. We also hope that they're watching over us on Earth.

I find it fascinating that even though angels are symbolized or somehow represented almost everywhere we look (for example, their images can been seen in church paintings, our home decor, and even as guardian-angel charms or trinkets in our cars), when someone talks about a vision involving an angel or other spiritual figure, it's somehow considered "fringe."

We've all heard about the mysterious Angel of Death, the scary being who arrives unnoticed and whisks us off into the darkness. But society's perception of this has been changing.

Take, for instance, the recent portrayal of the Angel of Death as a kind-spirited being in the popular TV series <u>Touched by an Angel.</u> Likewise, my close friend Marianne Williamson once remarked: "I used to think that it would be a terrible thing to behold, but I now realize that the Angel of Death would have to be God's most tender and understanding ally in order to be sent to us at such a significant, frightening juncture."

It's not necessary to debate the reality of angels and other deathbed phenomena. They're much more than simple entities that can be proved or disproved. They comfort us and offer us hope. They're part of a religious and spiritual belief system that many of us hold sacred. And although some like to think of angels as "New Age," references to them can be traced back to the Old Testament. For example, in the book of Genesis, God starts out using the word <u>I,</u> but then switches to <u>We.</u> Many interpret this as referring to the angels, who existed before creation.

There are those who firmly assert that no one dies alone; in fact, many cultures believe that from the moment of birth to the end of physical existence, we're in the presence of God and angels. In time, they'll help us transition to a purely spiritual existence; and they'll also be there for those we leave behind, reminding us that our loved ones exist beyond death.

I wanted to learn more about these extraordinary visions of God, angels, and heaven; and I couldn't help but wonder: Do any rabbis believe in these visions? Do priests or nuns witness these experiences? How do doctors, nurses, social workers, or hospital chaplains interpret spiritual visions?

The answers to those questions are in the following pages.

◆

Is This Heaven?

by Daryl

I've been a radiation oncologist for eight years. I became a doctor because my natural inclination has always been to help others. My mom had cancer when I was a teenager, and I played an integral role in taking care of her during her treatment and prolonged recovery. That experience impacted me greatly, and at 16, I got certified as a nursing assistant. I worked at a hospital for two consecutive summers while I was in high school, and continued on through college. When I was in medical school, I developed an enormous respect for health-care professionals, particularly when I assisted nurses in the oncology unit.

About 30 years after my mother's bout with cancer, she got sick again. I was an oncologist at that point and treated her at home for about six months. She died while I was caring for her, succumbing to radiation-induced colon cancer that was metastatic at diagnosis.

Physicians seem to have little understanding that their own attitudes toward death and dying strongly influence their practice patterns, including how they decide to prolong or withdraw treatment from their patients. I see a huge need in the oncology world—that is, among doctors, nurses, radiation technicians, therapists, and chemotherapy nurses—for a basic understanding of counseling skills. They all need to be more involved in end-of-life decisions and the dying process itself.

I remember a patient I once had named John, who had throat cancer. He'd been a heavy smoker and drinker in his younger years, but he'd recently developed a strong Baptist faith and abandoned his unhealthy lifestyle. I prescribed radiation therapy for him because he wasn't a surgical candidate; unfortunately, within a year after the treatment, the cancer returned.

John soon developed lymph-node disease as well as the cancer recurrence in his throat, which was gradually choking him. Even after all the treatment options were exhausted and John passed away, I was glad to have the opportunity to provide some of his supportive care. I got to know his wife, Nicole, pretty well, and I'll never forget the story she told me about the moment he died.

On John's last day, he went through the usual process of losing energy and going in and out of consciousness. He was air starved (feeling a shortness of breath), but a morphine drip was making him more comfortable. As Nicole hugged her husband, she could tell that death was imminent. John's breathing had slowed, and he was having agonal (shallow, slow, and irregular) respirations. She got into bed with him and gently held him. They were both looking at the ceiling when John told Nicole that he saw clouds above him.

After taking a final breath, he uttered, "I'm going through the clouds. Is this heaven?" Then he died in his wife's arms. Although fleeting, the vision was very powerful. Nicole was comforted that the clouds parted and heaven welcomed her husband, as if John's faith in eternal life was being validated for her.

This is only one of many stories I've heard or experienced firsthand throughout my career that go beyond a medical or scientific explanation.

• ◈ •

A VISIT FROM ABOVE

by Theodore

As a hospital chaplain, I never know what the day will bring. I consider my work to be about connecting patients to God in whatever form that may take: prayer, confession, discussion, Bible reading, and so on. Sometimes when people are sick, they naturally turn to a higher power; others forget that He is there, and I remind them. I want everyone to know that the Lord never leaves our side.

One day, I was called in to the ICU to spend time with a woman named Sally who was from out of state. She'd come to the area to visit her daughter, son-in-law, and only grandchild; but a few days after she arrived, her daughter noticed that her mother didn't seem well and brought her to the emergency room.

They immediately admitted her to the ICU, which wasn't a good sign. After numerous tests and workups, the doctors determined that Sally was experiencing multiple organ failure. She'd been fighting diabetes most of her life, and her kidneys hadn't been functioning properly. Now, as it often happens, a domino effect was occurring: as one organ began to fail, it put more strain on the others. Eventually, this patient's lungs, kidneys, heart, and liver were beginning to lose precious functions.

When I arrived, I was told that Sally wasn't expected to live much longer. I found the family outside in the waiting area, and told them that while helping her say good-bye was the hardest thing they'd ever have to do, it was also the most important.

It was about 10 A.M. when we went back to Sally's bedside. She was still awake and alert, but it was obvious that her body was rapidly shutting down. I was able to encourage the family to shower her with love and speak words of appreciation. Sally, who hadn't uttered a word in the last few hours, suddenly sat up and said in a clear voice, "Jesus, you're here."

I noticed that she was looking past me and slightly upward. Then she lay back down, saying, "It is done," and closed her eyes and was silent. Her daughter and I looked at each other, although neither of us said anything. It was obvious that we both felt we'd just witnessed something pure and profound. Within hours, Sally took her last breath and died.

Afterward, I approached the doctor who had treated her and asked, "Was Sally on any pain medication?"

"No, she wasn't," he replied, but then he assured me that if he'd seen any signs of her discomfort, he would have administered the necessary drugs.

"Was she on any medication that might have caused her to hallucinate?"

The doctor took a quick look at her chart and said that she wasn't. I pictured myself telling this story to colleagues and wanted to be a step ahead of any points they could conceivably bring up to discredit Sally's vision. If what she'd seen wasn't a result of medication, I thought that people would assume it was caused by a lack of oxygen, so I asked the doctor if she was at all oxygen deprived when I was with her.

Looking at me curiously, he remarked, "Okay, something's up. What are you getting at?"

I told him the story, and like a detective, he began to examine Sally's medical chart more closely. Her vitals had been compromised, but the pulse-oximeter reading had been satisfactory. The doctor then said, "I can tell you for sure that there were no medications administered that would have caused hallucinations, and her oxygen flow appeared adequate."

He paused a moment and continued. "Chaplain, you've said that you help people find God. Maybe today, Jesus found *her*, and you were just a witness. By the way, this happens all the time, but no one wants to talk about it."

"Why not?"

"Well, it's like this: I want other doctors to refer their patients to me; and I want to be seen as competent, technically astute, and on top of cutting-edge treatments. If I went around telling people that my patients were having deathbed visions, do you think I'd be taken seriously?"

He patted me on the back and smiled. "Now don't go telling the whole hospital we had this conversation."

I appreciated this doctor's kindness and the fact that he shared his secret with me. It's too bad that although many physicians acknowledge that visions occur, no one will talk about them. In the big picture, however, what mattered most was the expression on Sally's face when she saw Jesus. It was beautiful to see someone look so genuinely at peace. For me, that said it all.

◆

I Don't Question What Happens

by Daniel

Before I became a rabbi, I was an optometrist with a strong background in science. Years ago, if people had told me about deceased loved ones visiting their living relatives, I would have thought they were crazy. But times have changed, and I'm older and wiser. I know I don't have all the answers. All I know for sure is that rational men and women, whose words I'd believe in any other situation, tell these stories. They've taught me that the more I experience, the more I know deep in my heart that the soul lives on.

My story is about a member of my congregation named Aaron. At 92 years old, he was still very active in our temple. He resided at a nearby assisted-living facility and would walk over three to four times a week. He attended services every Friday night and would show up for most of the events we held, from speakers to classes, and he also loved playing cards.

Aaron had three brothers and one sister, and they'd all lived well into their 90s. He was the youngest, and although his brothers had all died, one had even reached 100 years old. His sister, Rose, was 94 and lived in a nursing home in Florida, but they hadn't seen each other in more than five years. Aaron said they'd been focused on their own children and grandchildren, and he and his sister only spoke once or twice a year.

One day I noticed that Aaron seemed unsteady on his feet. His visits to the temple became less frequent, and eventually, I only saw him on Friday nights. The decline occurred over a two-year period, and he explained to me that he just didn't have the energy anymore. At his age, I didn't think that was unusual.

Around this time, Aaron's eldest daughter, who had dinner with him every Sunday, told me that she'd noticed that her father's appetite wasn't what it used to be. After noting that he also seemed to be losing weight, she took him to the doctor—and after a number of tests, the news wasn't good. The doctors suspected cancer and wanted to hospitalize Aaron for further testing. He objected, saying, "It's just getting a bit harder for me to walk, and I'm not hungry that often. My body is telling me that my life is almost over, and I have no complaints. I've been lucky! I have a daughter, two sons, and five beautiful grandkids. What more do I need?"

His daughter pleaded with him not to give up. With a smile, he told her, "No one gives up at 92. It might be considered giving up at 75, but I'm approaching the finish line of this race. I can see it and you should, too. Many people my age are in nursing homes like my sister, Rose. Attempting chemo in your 90s may be an option for some, but it isn't for me."

The doctor prescribed a medication to help increase Aaron's appetite, but six months after his 93rd birthday, he really began to decline. His children took him to the doctor to run additional tests to see if there was anything else going on. The doctor still suspected cancer, but believed that it was slow growing. In addition, a test revealed that Aaron's heart was weak, and he needed a pacemaker. He objected again, and this time the doctor didn't try to argue. Between a weakened heart and his other health issues, there was no getting this elderly fellow back to his old self.

Within two months, Aaron was on his deathbed, and his daughter and sons were by his side. One day when he was resting, they all heard him say, "Rose, you're here."

His children exchanged confused glances, and his daughter asked, "Dad, are you talking about Aunt Rose? She's in a nursing home in Florida—remember?"

He paid no attention; instead, he smiled and said, "Rose, you're here! It must be time for us to go."

Aaron died shortly thereafter. When his daughter called to break the news to her cousin in Florida, she found out that her aunt Rose had died in her sleep the night before.

The family was shocked. They turned to me, their rabbi, wondering if it was possible that their aunt had really come to visit their father on his deathbed. "Why not?" I responded. "It's possible. She'd already passed when he had the vision."

They all seemed skeptical. I explained that they could spend their lives questioning it, but why not just accept it as part of their father's dying experience?

Then the eldest son spoke up, saying, "Well, we don't need to be telling anyone else about this."

"Why not?"

"Rabbi, my father was a good man, a smart man. I don't want his last words to make others think he was crazy."

"Your father was an incredible man who lived a wonderful life. I'd hate for his last moment to be labeled by anyone as 'crazy.' I see the concern on your face, but I don't want you to think he had a weird experience that you'll now have to keep secret or feel ashamed of. That isn't who Aaron was. *I* believe that Rose came to him."

"But there's no logical explanation for this."

"I don't question what happens," I replied. "I just pay attention to it. Do you think people would question *me* if I talked about someone's vision?"

"No. They'd believe you."

"With all of your permission, I'd like to tell the story of who Aaron was at his memorial. I'd love to talk about his integrity, his generosity, his belief in his family, and his love of Judaism. But I also want to bring up his vision, and I want all of you to watch everyone's reactions."

The family consented.

During the funeral service, I talked about Aaron's life and shared how Judaism says many things about the afterlife, including "from dust to dust," reincarnation, and the Kabbalistic approach. Just as there are Conservative, Orthodox, and Reform Jews, there are numerous interpretations of what happens when we die. Then I went into the story of Aaron's vision of Rose and explained that over the years, several families have shared similar stories with me that they were afraid to tell others. Then I asked the congregation, "How many of you have ever witnessed or heard of someone being visited by a deceased loved one?"

The room was packed with more than a hundred mourners, and Aaron's family watched as many hands raised and heads nodded, confirming that they'd also had this experience. After the service, I told Aaron's children how many people had approached me and shared their stories.

It seems that we tend to isolate ourselves when we could be more deeply connected to our friends and families. We want to know that our lives continue after we're gone. I assured Aaron's daughter and sons that their father's "story" didn't end at death, and neither did Rose's. Perhaps he'd even come back to greet his own children when it's their time.

•◇•

GETTING YOUR HOUSE IN ORDER

by Katherine

After I got my master's degree in counseling, I began volunteering with a cancer support program. I decided to specialize in that area, and today I work in a private oncology outpatient center. My experience with a deathbed vision left me with a mixture of sadness and wonder.

I'm not a religious or spiritual person, but I've always felt connected to my patients and understood their struggle. My greatest life lesson, however, came from my grandfather Bob.

When my grandpa came down with pulmonary fibrosis (a lung disease, which, in his case, was terminal), I helped take care of him during the last six weeks of his life. I was a counselor and hadn't worked in the hospice setting, so this was my first time caring for someone who was actively dying.

I'd never really gotten to know my very devout grandfather. My parents, who were not religious, had been killed in a car accident when I was 24. Since then, I felt like I'd lost touch with my family, but helping my grandmother and her two sisters was my chance to reconnect.

As my grandfather's health declined, I tried to keep up with his condition so I'd know what to expect. Since I love to read, each time I saw a change in him, I'd look up whatever symptom he was exhibiting in the moment. I also noticed that as he got closer to death, he seemed to withdraw from his loved ones.

My grandmother was taking it really hard, but she didn't want to talk about her feelings. Then one day, Grandpa kept saying something about "cleaning up the house" and "getting the house in order." At first, I thought he meant that he wanted me to clean up his room, which was immaculate, so

I gently said, "Grandpa, the floor is clean, and everything is in its place."

"No, Katherine—that's not what I mean."

He didn't say anything else. Shortly afterward, his doctor told us that he wouldn't last through the week, but he hung on. I think he must have felt that we needed more time to adjust to his death.

One day, my grandfather started talking about one of his brothers who had already died and said that he was actually standing in the corner of the room. "I've got to get this house in order," my grandpa repeated. I wasn't sure that cleaning things up and getting the house in order were the same thing, but he kept talking about both of them, saying that he didn't have a lot of time left.

Grandpa had a hard time sleeping, and we were all exhausted from staying up all night when he was awake. We were worried that he might get up when one of us was napping, so we hired a nurse's aide named Hilda to help us out.

One evening we were sitting by my grandfather, and he started to once again look in the corner of the room and talk about getting his house in order. Hilda glanced over at me, and I immediately told her, "He does that all the time—talking about getting his house in order and cleaning things up. Don't worry, we don't want you to do any housecleaning."

Looking at me strangely, she replied, "He's quoting a passage from the Bible."

"Really?!" I was curious and embarrassed all at once.

"Yes, it's from the Old Testament. Isaiah the prophet came to Hezekiah and said, 'The Lord says, set your house in order, for you shall die and not live.'"

"So that's what he means by getting his house in order. My grandpa used to be a minister; it makes sense that he'd recite from the Bible."

"Ministers need to get their houses in order to die just like everyone else. Have you noticed if he's looked over at one particular spot in the room?" she inquired

"Yes, he's been doing that, too. How did you know?"

"A lot of dying people do this. Do you know what the rest of the Bible passage he was quoting says?"

"I haven't a clue," I responded.

"'Hezekiah turned his face to the wall and prayed to the Lord.'"

"So this is a religious thing?"

"Not necessarily. Watch your grandfather the next time he's talking about getting his house in order and looking in the corner of the room. I bet that he isn't really looking at the wall—he's seeing something beyond."

"Do some people refer to this when they're dying because it's in the Bible, or is it in the Bible because that's exactly what happens when we die?"

"I don't think folks do it for any particular reason," Hilda mused. "It's just something that happens. People who are dying often see God, Jesus, or even their relatives who have already passed away."

After Hilda's explanation, it all seemed so profound. I told my grandfather that I was certain his house was in order. I asked him if I could do anything to help, and he said, "No, honey. I almost have it all done."

I stayed quiet after that because I sensed that Grandpa was dealing with a world that I couldn't see or be a part of. When I told him how much I'd miss him, he replied, "You and the rest of the family will all be okay."

He then starting talking to his brother, saying, "I know what you're doing here." None of us dismissed it (thank goodness for Hilda's explanation), but some friends who stopped by or other family members were blaming it on the medication he was taking. I knew that wasn't the case, though.

As my grandfather grew weaker, he spoke less and less often. During his final hours of life, we told him how much we loved him, and shortly before he died, I remarked, "It looks like your house is in order."

He smiled. I have no doubt that I'd experienced something that's beyond this world.

Dinner with an Angel

by Matt

My brother, Brian, who was only 35 years old, was dying of AIDS at his home.

He had enjoyed a lot of success in his career. A heating, ventilating, and air-conditioning engineer, he'd worked closely with architects in order to design systems that didn't interfere with a building's look . . . but that was now in the past. My brother's condition was quickly deteriorating, and it was an intense time because I knew that he wouldn't be around much longer.

One night Brian was feeling well enough and asked if we could go out for some Chinese food. His nurse, Gloria, and I knew that getting him there wouldn't be easy, but we also knew that this could be one of the last times we ever took him anywhere. He could have asked to go anywhere or do anything, but he wanted to go to a restaurant for Chinese food, and we were determined to make it happen.

When we were seated at the restaurant, we ordered a bunch of different dishes so Brian could taste everything. I cut his food up like he was a child and helped him eat. He was pretty weak but loved being out of the house. Then, out of the blue, he began reaching away from the table, as if he were trying to grab something. I feel ashamed to admit that at first I treated him like a distracted little kid, saying, "There's nothing there—your food is here!" I got up and gently turned him back toward the table, but he immediately turned away again, staring intently at something.

"Brian, what is it? What are you looking at?" I asked.

He was transfixed, but then he had the widest smile on

his face. I glanced over to where I thought he was staring but didn't see anything. What on earth was I missing?

"What is it?!" I repeated.

"Look!" he exclaimed. "She's in white. I've never seen anything so white."

"Who? Who's in white?"

"*She* is!"

"There's no one there, Brian. You're looking at the wall, and it's not even a white wall!"

Thankfully, Gloria jumped in, saying, "Wow! Tell us more about her."

"She's an angel—a real angel." I noticed that my brother's face was suddenly very relaxed, but I was kind of embarrassed by his behavior. Here we were in a restaurant, and he was claiming to see an angel dressed in all white. All I could think was, *Check, please!*

Gloria put her hand on mine. "It's okay," she said. "These things happen when people are leaving. They see angels and visions. There's nothing to be afraid of or feel ashamed about. In nursing and in hospice, we see this all the time."

Brian spent the rest of our dinner staring peacefully at the angel. I looked around periodically, but no one seemed to notice what my brother was doing—or if they did, they didn't care.

I turned to Gloria and asked, "Do you think dying people might be looking for something at the end of the road, when time is running out? Maybe they don't know what has happened, but when they hit that wall at the end, they ask if anyone's there. They want to know where they're going. Is that why they see visions of angels?"

"I just don't question it anymore. I used to, but it seems to happen so often—if patients are on medication, off medication, minutes before death, and even a few weeks before death. I'm sorry to break this to you, Matt, but if your brother is seeing angels, he'll be with them soon. People think that because he has AIDS, he won't be in heaven, but if she came to him, that's proof enough for me."

"I wonder if even the most faithful person in the world questions a vision of Jesus."

Gloria perked up. "That's interesting," she said. "I used to think that someone who was very religious would surely believe in their loved ones seeing a vision of Jesus or an angel, but that's not always the case."

After noticing that Brian had turned back to the table and was eating, I continued my chat with Gloria. "I think when people are dying, they have a million feelings going on inside that they don't know how to identify. There's just no way to process them all, so they envision something comforting like an angel or a loved one—but I still don't think he saw something real."

"I'm done," Brian said suddenly. "We can go home now— that was wonderful."

"You've always enjoyed your food," I said lovingly.

"Oh, not the food. I meant the angel was wonderful."

Just before we all got up, I leaned toward Gloria and whispered, "I'm still a skeptic."

My brother passed away three days later.

•◇•

The Last Face You See

by Patty

For more than 30 years now, I've worked in hospice and facilitated a support group for people who have lost their spouses. I mainly teach bereavement classes and workshops.

I'll never forget how my life was forever changed the day my husband, Jason, died at the age of 25. We lived in a small town in Montana where there was no such thing as support groups for grieving husbands and wives. There, nobody knew what to do or say to a 25-year-old widow with a seven-month-old son. But I was thrust into this world when another car broadsided Jason's car, killing him instantly.

My story about a vision involves a woman I met when I gave a one-day workshop in Illinois on grief and bereavement. This woman approached me at lunch and showed me a picture of her daughter, Julie, who had died at the age of 12. She was born with multiple disabilities and had endured countless surgeries during her short life. By the time she was nearing death, she was partially paralyzed and spending her days in a wheelchair or in bed. One of her disabilities prevented her from speaking, but she'd learned sign language, so she and her parents could communicate.

In the last week or so before Julie died, her mother noticed that she'd often look up toward the corner of the room and break into this huge glowing smile. She'd wave her hand as if she were greeting her very best friend whom she hadn't seen in a long time. She just looked so excited, so thrilled. Her mother would try to ask her what was going on, but Julie was too absorbed by whatever she was seeing and didn't notice her mom signing. When Julie would "come back," it was as if she'd been in another place.

Her mother would ask, "What did you see?"

Julie's response was always: "Didn't you see? Jesus was here! Didn't you see him?"

This happened at least three or four times. When Julie wasn't seeing the vision of Jesus, she'd sign things to her mother, such as: "Did you know that Jesus comes to take children to heaven? He comes and makes everyone better."

Her mother didn't think that anyone would believe this, so the next time her daughter was experiencing the vision and had that beautiful, glowing smile on her face, she took a picture of her. And that was the photo she showed me that day at my workshop. It truly was remarkable: this emaciated, tiny girl sitting in her wheelchair and looking up toward the corner. I've seen happy children. I've see kids who see their grandparents and light up and wave, but there was something different about Julie's expression. She had an otherworldly look, like an angel seeing heaven. It was just amazing.

That encounter provided me with a lot of comfort and peace about my own husband. I hope that in his final moments, the last face he saw wasn't the driver in the car about to hit him. I hope the last face he saw on Earth was Jesus's. In that brief flash, Jason wasn't just a man dying in a car accident who had a young wife and child at home; he was a man who was being taken home to heaven.

I've heard many similar accounts from colleagues. Almost without exception, everyone starts his or her story with something like: "I've never told anybody this, and if I did, they'd put me in the nuthouse—but this is what I experienced. . . ."

These are genuine, profound moments. Whenever I feel sad, I envision the picture of that smiling, glowing little girl and envision my husband with that same heavenly grin.

◆

BLINDED BY THE LIGHT

by Sue

I completed a year of internship as a social worker and then started a job at a hospice. I wanted to work with the dying for as long as I could remember—my motivation being the death of my mother in a car accident when I was two years old.

I'd spent my life wondering about this woman I never knew. When I was a teenager and my friends were constantly fighting with their mothers, I kept my mouth shut because I knew that I'd give anything to be able to have an argument with my own mom. Whenever I told my pals how much I missed her, they'd always say, "You're lucky to only have one parent getting mad and punishing you!" I knew that my loss was more than the average teenager could ever comprehend, though. When I reached adulthood, my curiosity about my mother didn't diminish in the least. I'd ask every relative and every one of her friends what she was like, trying to piece together the life of this person who'd died before I ever got the chance to know her.

One day I decided to investigate a bit further and read my mom's autopsy report—the final document about her life. "Blunt trauma" and "internal bleeding" were listed as "cause of death," but none of that offered me anything meaningful. When I told the clerk there that I wanted the "whys" and "hows" of my mother's death, she told me that many people were interested in such things. It was normal, she added, and it seemed to make a person feel better to learn the facts of what happened to a loved one. In this case, all I knew was that my mother had lost control of her car and apparently had been blinded by another car's high beams.

Considering my history, it was hardly surprising that I ended up working in hospice care. I somehow felt at home working with dying people and their families. One patient named Jarrod really stands out in my mind.

Jarrod was close to death, and I was spending some time with his family when I felt a sudden urge to go to his room. Standing in front of the window, I gently whispered his name.

"You're blocking my light," Jarrod responded.

I quickly moved over when I realized that he wasn't facing the window at all. In fact, Jarrod was staring at the wall. "Can you see better now?" I asked, curious. "Do you see the light?"

"Yes!" he exclaimed, looking upward and off to the right. I looked at the spot where Jarrod was focused to see if a mirror or shiny object was creating a reflection, but there was nothing there—just the empty corner of the room.

"Tell me about the light," I urged him.

"Oh, it's so beautiful, so blinding, I can barely see."

"What else?"

"So beautiful," he repeated, as I moved closer to him. "Blinding," he whispered.

Those were Jarrod's last words. He died minutes later, appearing comfortable and at peace.

I was stunned and upset, though. I'd heard from nurses how their patients had seen visions, angels, and bright lights before they died, but I was still unnerved. As I continued with my hospice work, however, I soon became aware that these events were part and parcel of the very fabric of end-of-life care.

One day, many years after Jarrod had died, I was with my father. For some reason, I felt compelled to ask him to tell me again what he remembered about my mother's accident.

"She was driving home from a friend's house and must have lost control of the car during the rain," he replied. "We lived in the mountains, and a storm could make those curvy roads very dangerous."

"So it was the headlights from the car in the opposite direction that blinded her?"

"Well, the truth is we don't know if there *was* another car." My father paused and sighed. "I talked with the first paramedic who was on the scene, and he said that your mom kept talking about a blinding light. He assumed that it must have been a car's headlights."

I thought back to Jarrod and remembered the look of peace on his face when he saw the light, and I recalled that he'd repeated the word *blinding*. For the first time, I finally felt like I was getting an answer to my lifelong search. Perhaps my mother hadn't seen a car's lights at all—instead, she'd gazed upon that same beautiful, shining light that Jarrod had seen as he died.

•◇•

A Surprising Visit

by Sofia

My father and I are both social workers. I work in a hospital system, and he was the CEO of an outpatient-counseling program. I'm so proud of my dad, who'd been honored at the White House for his contributions to mental-health care. In addition, my mother was an accomplished professor who had a Ph.D. in mathematics.

Can you imagine growing up with a mother who had a Ph.D. in math? It was intense, but I have to say that she was a great teacher and made my homework fun. I would have loved to have taken after her, but I didn't inherit the math gene. Instead, I saw my father as more of a role model, and since I was always pretty comfortable around people, I thought social work would be a good fit for me.

Life was good until my mother was diagnosed with an aggressive cancer. She began chemotherapy, and lost her hair and experienced terrible nausea. Many months passed and she showed no promising results at all. We were heartbroken as we watched her go through so much suffering, but we didn't turn to the church. Although we were a family of Christians, we were hardly religious and rarely attended service. We just tried to be good people, and sometimes we prayed together.

Eventually, Mom's drastic decline made us aware that the chemotherapy was not working. The doctors were stumped, saying they'd done all they could. That was when Mom decided to seek hospice care at our home.

A few weeks later, my father and I noticed that my mother was acting severely agitated. When the hospice nurse came for her daily visit, Dad asked her, "Why does my wife seem so upset lately?"

"This is common," the nurse explained. "We call it 'terminal agitation,' and it sometimes happens at the end of life."

"I've heard about that," I offered, nodding to my dad and trying to be the daughter rather than the social worker.

For the next few days, Mom constantly drifted in and out of consciousness. Yet she didn't appear to be at peace, showing signs of continuing agitation. She also rarely spoke, just saying a few words here and there. One afternoon when Dad and I were both at her bedside, Mom came out of a total silence, opened her eyes, and said quite clearly, "Oh, I just saw Jesus."

All of us (including my mom) were genuinely surprised by her vision. I mean, we always thought of ourselves as "Christian-lite," hardly pious enough to get a home visit from Jesus! But that seemed to be exactly what my mother was seeing.

At the time, Dad and I didn't really stop to think about what we believed. We just focused on Mom and how shocked she was. It was obvious that she didn't know how to process her vision, because it was so outside of her reality. My father comforted her immediately, saying, "Well, if you saw Jesus, then I guess he must have seen you, too."

I thought that was a smart thing for Dad to say. Rather than trying to reorient Mom to our reality, he just acknowledged hers and didn't try to take it away. His only concern was keeping his wife as comfortable as possible during this time.

A few days later when Mom died, she was much more at peace. I believe that these types of visions can absolutely be real because I don't know for sure that they're *not* real. I think there's something much greater than myself, and if I'm open to it, maybe it will bring me peace, too.

Dad and I came away from this experience with a deeper sense of faith. When I realized that Mom was being comforted by Jesus and was on her way to heaven, I felt that she was well taken care of, and I didn't have to worry about her anymore.

As I explore an area as broad as deathbed visions, it's comforting to know that this phenomenon doesn't exist separately from spirituality. Visions of angels, God, and other spiritual figures reassure me that we don't travel this path alone. The next subject matter I'll explore will add even more richness to the concept of this life as a journey.

CHAPTER SEVEN

THE JOURNEY OF
THE DYING—A TRIP
OF A LIFETIME

*"I have a long journey to take,
and must bid the company farewell."*
— final words of Sir Walter Raleigh

The second commonly shared deathbed experience is getting ready for a "trip." This is nicely illustrated in Mark's story:

Mark, who was one of my patients, was always the head of the family, a take-charge kind of guy. From coaching the kids' baseball games when they were young to running his own company, he was prepared. During his long battle with cancer, he played an active role with his physician in deciding which chemotherapy treatment was right for him. When he realized that he wasn't getting better, he quickly changed the agenda and started planning for his death. He made sure that his family was aware of his wishes and even walked his loving wife through the details of his funeral arrangements.

When he became bedbound, the family spent time sharing old memories and telling Mark that he was a wonderful father and husband. As the long days went by, he began sleeping more and more. He'd wake up and ask for water, but he always shook his head no if they asked him if he was in pain. Hours before his death, his opened his eyes wide and asked his wife, "Is everything ready?"

Not knowing what to say, she responded, "Mark, we're all here."

"Are my bags packed?"

"What bags, dear?"

"The bags for my trip—it's almost time to go."

His wife attributed his confusion to his pain medication. She was unaware that her husband, like so many others close to death, was overcome by a need to prepare for an impending journey.

This phenomenon isn't new or unusual. In many people's final hours, they regard their impending death as an actual physical voyage—that is, they don't really associate it with dying. I've never heard my patients say, "I have to pack my bags for my trip into death!" In their minds, the transition is still associated with life. Even though dying is the trip of a lifetime, that connection just isn't made.

Most individuals don't realize that this sense of taking a journey is actually a part of the history of end-of-life care. In fact, during the Middle Ages, a hospice was actually a way station where people could find a safe haven, a small oasis while on the road. Travelers were afforded the opportunity to rest and reenergize before they resumed their long, wearisome treks to unknown destinations. Those who were truly at death's door were also welcomed and provided with bedding, food, and companionship. While we don't tend to think about the origin of our modern-day hospices, the archetype remains embedded in our subconsciousness—the act of dying may be the rest we need before our final journey.

This phenomenon can take many forms for an individual. For some, it may be about packing their bags and getting their tickets, while for others it's all in preparing themselves "to go." Certain diseases, such as terminal cancer, have a very clear trajectory, with peaks and valleys and a predictable decline at the end. Other illness, such as heart and lung diseases, may have periods of compromised health and then sudden death. The way in which we die definitely impacts how we prepare for the journey. This brings to mind another patient of mine:

Arthur was an active man in his late 50s who had lived with lung disease for the last decade of his life. In the past few weeks, he'd been feeling fatigued and was using his oxygen more and more while staying close to home. One morning, however, he woke up with a burst of energy, showered, shaved, and put on his favorite suit and tie. When he called a couple of friends to pick him up for breakfast, they were surprised to see him so dressed up. They asked if anything special was going on, and he replied, "I woke up feeling good and just had a sense that today is going to be different."

They all enjoyed a great breakfast, and Arthur's friends were glad to see him up and about. When he returned home, he felt like taking a nap. He hung up his suit jacket neatly, lay down on his bed, and then died.

Arthur's friends weren't too shocked by his death since they'd been expecting it. At first they were taken off guard by the way he'd meticulously groomed himself for breakfast, but later they acknowledged that some folks wear sweats on airplanes and some wear suits. Arthur was clearly the latter: he made sure that he looked neat and put together for his final trip.

To us, these "trips" may seem to be all about leaving, but for the dying, they may be more about arriving. This chapter gives us more insight into such stories.

THE BOAT IS AT THE PIER

by Anita

As a social worker in a major hospital, my job is to listen to my patients' experiences, identify their resources, and help direct them through the complex medical system. I'd like to share a story about Felicia, who was in her 80s and dying of congestive heart failure. An attractive woman with long gray hair, she was a homemaker who had raised her children, who now had children of their own. Her husband had worked in the oil fields and provided well for the family.

Felicia had been a lively, energetic woman for most of her life, and she'd suffered from few illnesses. When she was diagnosed with heart disease, she played it down, sure that her doctors were overreacting.

I'd rarely seen this woman sick or even tired, so although her condition worsened, she remained in denial for as long as possible. It was easy to do so, since Felicia could easily conceal the few health problems she was experiencing. But soon she couldn't hide it anymore, since simply breathing was getting harder every day. When Felicia started to feel fatigued, her daughter, Carole, took her to a health-food store and bought vitamins, protein drinks, and raw foods. Felicia indulged her by taking all of it, but nothing restored her energy and sense of well-being.

Over a period of six months, Felicia stopped going out with friends, preferring to just talk on the phone. But as time went by, her breathing became even more labored. She'd have to pause at inappropriate times in a conversation in order to inhale, and her friends and family started to worry. Felicia became incredibly frustrated because instead of listening to what she was saying, they were listening to her breathing and could only talk about her illness. She once told her friend Joan: "I'm having trouble catching my breath—I know that. Now can we get past that and just talk?"

Shortly thereafter, Felicia stopped taking calls altogether because it was so frustrating and tiring. Carole was concerned because her mom had always been a social butterfly, and her life was once all about playing bridge and going to the movies with friends. But all that stopped.

A few months later, Felicia stopped talking completely, not because her hearing was diminishing or that she just didn't want to, but because even the simple act of speaking exhausted her beyond belief. When it was clear to everyone that she was very close to dying, her family gathered and took turns watching over her. I was there to provide them with whatever assistance I could. She continued her silence until one day she suddenly sat up, very primlike, and waved at her daughter to look toward where she was pointing.

"Don't you see them?" Felicia asked. Her voice sounded clear as a bell, and her breathing was steady and even for the first time in many months.

"See who?"

"I see a dock; and there are your dad, grandmother, grandfather, and uncle."

Felicia's brother had died many years ago, when he was in his 20s; her husband had died of a heart attack when he was in his 70s, about a decade previously.

"I still don't see them," Carole said.

"Well, they're all there!" her mother exclaimed. "They're standing on the dock, waiting for me to come across." She paused, and then spoke directly to those she was gazing upon: "There's no boat at the dock. How can I get to you?"

Carole had no clue how to answer her. I didn't know what to say myself, but I did know that Felicia's question wasn't for us and that she'd find the answer when the time came.

The following day, Felicia quietly uttered, "The boat is finally at the pier." Those were her last words. In the end, she died peacefully.

◆

THE RIGHT BUS

by Gwen

I work at an institute that primarily helps people with disabilities live normal lives. One of the clients who grew up under our care was a spirited young woman named Sharon who wanted to help others. A kind soul and a dynamic presence, we often asked her to speak on behalf of people with disabilities who deserved equal access and treatment without discrimination.

Sharon's challenge was an intellectual disability; unable to care for her, her parents had her institutionalized in a large mental hospital as a child. By that, I mean she was labeled as "mentally retarded," but at the time, it was a catchall phrase for many conditions that had no mandatory education attached or accurate testing to distinguish one disability from the other.

Sharon was transferred to a group home, but eventually she was able to live on her own in an apartment. She had diabetes throughout most of her life, and by the time she reached her 40s, it was getting quite serious and debilitating. As she was nearing her final days, she began to talk about waiting for a bus. (Although she wasn't able to drive, this remarkable woman was very independent and took the bus wherever she needed to go.)

Sharon was confined to her bed due to the complications from diabetes, and she began talking more and more about the bus she was waiting for. Because of her intellectual disability, her family and friends assumed that she was confused or hallucinating and discounted her, even though she was never on any pain medication.

My client continued to tell anyone who'd listen about the bus she needed, but she also started mentioning other buses that had stopped to pick her up but weren't the right ones. She brought this up when I was with her one day, so I asked her which was the right bus. She responded, "It needs to be accessible . . . it needs a ramp."

When I mentioned that she didn't need a ramp because she didn't use a wheelchair, Sharon said, "The right one will have a ramp. All the good buses have ramps." And then she told me, "I'll get on the right bus—it will be *my* bus." Shortly before she died, at the age of 52, I saw her light up and look very happy. "It's here!" she said with delight. "It's the right bus, and it has a ramp."

I've worked with enough people who have terminal conditions and illnesses to know that sometimes they talk about going on a trip when they're about to die. It doesn't necessarily have anything to do with how they moved around in life. In Sharon's case, she insisted that the "right bus" would have a ramp, but I don't think it had anything to do with her disability—it was all about her transition. I think the ramp symbolized accessibility to her.

To this day, I believe that Sharon got on the *right* bus. Because her life was about helping others, making sure they were granted equal rights despite their perceived limitations, in her final days, she became an advocate for herself. Obviously, she'd found the right bus with the right people on it for her.

· ◇ ·

I'M GOING ON A RIDE

by Margaret

Today, I work in a crisis-intervention center, but I'll never forget my days as a social worker at a children's hospital. I fondly remember a little girl named Teresa who was about six years old and had a very aggressive form of cystic fibrosis.

Teresa was kind and gentle; she also had a fragility that made other kids want to take care of her and was well loved. Unfortunately, as she checked into the hospital this time, there was a sense that she might not make it out. It was a hard thing to predict, but her lungs were pretty shot.

At one point, she asked for her dolls from home. She'd brought two dolls with her, but made it clear to her mother that *all* of them needed to be there with her. She'd never asked for this before. A bit concerned, her mom agreed and went home to gather them up. And she had quite a haul to make, since Teresa had every doll and stuffed animal imaginable. Each was loved by this little girl and given a name and a story.

As Teresa's condition worsened, she started to give her dolls away to other sick kids. Her mom was concerned and asked her what she'd do when she got home and had none of her old companions.

"Mommy," Teresa replied, "I'm not going to that home again. I'm going on a ride, and my dolls can't come with me."

Her mother was startled and didn't know what to say. She just watched her daughter give away her dolls and stuffed animals, one by one. The other kids, who seemed to understand that she was dying, would try to comfort Teresa's mom, saying things like, "We sure hope she gets better soon so we can give the dolls back."

When Teresa's breathing became more labored, she told her mom that she'd see her "at home."

"I'll make your favorite meal!" her mother exclaimed. "Burgers and banana cream pie! And everyone will bring your dolls over for you so you can take care of them again."

Teresa hugged her and softly replied, "I'm not going to need my dolls anymore, Mommy. I want everyone else to keep them because I have to go to another home now. You'll be there, too, but I have to go soon."

•◇•

TIME TO GET OFF THE FIELD

by Emily

In a hospice where I'd volunteered for many years, I had a patient named Murphy, a brilliant man who had Alzheimer's. He'd been a high-school football coach and loved talking about the game. In fact, he'd become very animated whenever he and I chatted about our favorite teams.

He loved watching NFL games on Sundays, and I enjoyed seeing how happy he was sitting by the TV in the common room of the hospice. He may not have known who I was sometimes (as a result of the disease), but he knew when a game was on.

As his health declined, Murphy got out to the common room less and less. And when he could no longer leave his room at all, I brought him a small portable TV so he could still watch the games. While most of the people around Murphy didn't pay a whole lot of attention to him, he and I spent time together and chatted right up to the day he passed away.

On his last day of life, I was with Murphy in his room. The TV was off, and he was quiet (and didn't seem to be in any pain). Then he suddenly said, "It's time to get off the field."

"What do you mean?"

"Game over."

"Are you upset that you've missed a game?" I asked.

"I'm not talking about football," he replied.

I knew this was significant. I called Murphy's family to tell them what happened and asked them to come.

They arrived, and sure enough, Murphy was moments from dying. He repeated, "Game over," one more time. He died peacefully that day, and I knew exactly what he'd meant.

◆

A Tough Old Bird

by Gail

I've worked in office management for years at a hospice center and have seen firsthand how illnesses and diseases can wreak havoc on families. Having grown up in New Orleans, what stands out most in my mind is seeing footage of hospital patients being rushed to safety during Hurricane Katrina in 2005.

I've seen many families weather storms, but no one was prepared for Katrina. More important to me, my 94-year-old father, Douglas, was still living in the area at the time. Although he made it through okay, I decided to move back to the city to be closer to him and my other family members. I still recall the events that led up to my move.

My dad was interviewed by a CNN reporter who was talking to locals about the disaster. He explained that when he returned home from the shelter, he'd spent several days alone with no electricity and little food and water. Fortunately, he was able to maintain telephone contact with the outside world.

The interviewer expressed her concern about his well-being, but my father responded, "I've lived through a heck of a lot already. I'm all right, but a lot of folks here need help."

I caught the interview on TV and laughed when the reporter referred to my dad as "a 94-year-old who's a tough old bird." He certainly was! But it was still a very difficult situation for him.

For my father's next birthday, he asked to go to the Fair Grounds Race Course but couldn't believe it when I told him that the racetrack hadn't reopened yet. He made me take him there so he could see for himself.

As we were driving around the empty parking lot, I was about to make a U-turn when Dad spotted a security guard and started waving at him. He turned to me, saying, "I haven't lived this long to not get the whole truth on a situation." He got out and asked the guard about what damage had happened to the track during the hurricane and when it was expected to reopen. He was disappointed that the guard couldn't give him a definite date and seemed dejected on the drive home. Spending time with his buddies at the Fair Grounds had been one of my father's favorite pastimes, and now a huge void had been created in his life.

Dad did his best to come to terms with the devastation of his beloved city, and the racetrack was one more piece of evidence that things were forever changed. The next year was hard for him, and little did we know that the one after that would be his last.

Although my dad was a fiercely independent man, he was getting weaker and his health was rapidly declining. He recognized his situation, pointing out, "I'm going on 96. That's the way it is—nothing's wrong."

Unfortunately, my family and I soon learned that Dad's prostate cancer, which he fought 13 years earlier, had returned. He also had an embolism in his left leg. He chose not to have surgery and also objected to any more invasive tests.

The physician didn't argue with my father, saying, "I could run more tests and start a few treatments, but your life is winding down. What do you want to do?"

"I've seen a lot! I've had so many loved ones die, and I know that we can't stay here forever," Dad replied. "My time is almost up, and there's no medicine that can change that."

My father began spending all his time with family, and we'd drive him all around New Orleans. It felt like he was reviewing the city to firmly cement it in his memory.

Eventually, the doctor told us it was time for Dad to seek hospice care. Of course, I was familiar with this arena, and I thought it made sense for him to be where he could be well taken care of.

Once we got him settled, my dad would rest a lot. He was also the perfect patient: cooperative, happy, and accepting. He continued telling us "Daddy stories," sharing anecdotes and life lessons with his children throughout his final days. It's as if he wanted to impart all his wisdom to us before passing on.

When the end was near, a family member was with him at all times. One night when I slept over, he suddenly woke up with a sense of urgency and exclaimed, "Gail, it's time to go!"

"Go where?"

"Out! Let's make a run for it—I have to be free."

Dad was insistent, but I wasn't sure how to answer. I decided to go along with it, telling him, "Okay, Dad. The car is outside. What do we do next?"

"Help me sit up."

I raised him up in bed and got him to the edge with his feet dangling. That's when he said, "Honey, I love you, but I can't stay here any longer. It's time for me to get going. Is the car ready?"

"It's right outside the door, Dad."

"Good. I'm ready. Are you?"

"Um, where are we going?"

"I'm not positive. I only know that I've got this trip in front of me, and the time has come."

I couldn't help but read between the lines. "I don't want you to go, Dad," I replied, looking into his beautiful brown eyes and blinking back tears.

He put his arms around me and sighed. "I know, honey, but I have to leave."

I clung to this tender moment, although I was afraid.

When my father leaned back onto his bed, I wasn't sure what to expect. He said, "Very soon—I just need to rest for a bit."

I gently helped him settle back into bed. "Dad, I don't think I'm going on the trip with you. I'll miss you while you're gone, but I'll be okay."

"You're right, honey. I can't take you with me, but I promise we'll see each other again."

During the predawn hours, my father was lying in bed with both arms extended toward the ceiling; it was as if he were reaching for something. I wondered what or whom he was seeing. Was it my grandmother, his mother? Could it be my own mother, his wife, who had died several years earlier? Had they come to take him on this "trip"?

Dad passed later that same morning at 9:50 A.M. at the age of 95. I believe that's when he began his trip into forever.

After listening to these stories, I was even more convinced that we cross a threshold when we die: a symbolic journey is completed, and the body comes to an end. Yet who we are seems to live on and continue traveling.

In my first book, The Needs of the Dying, I talked about the days when we used to be able to walk someone right up to his or her gate at the airport. Seeing our friends and family members off safely was an act of love, even if we were sad to see them go.

Similarly, we can walk beside our loved ones as they reach the end of their lives, but then we must let go. Yet do they ultimately die alone? Are there family and friends at their destination—the "gate" on the other side—just as anxious to greet them? Do they ever let us get a glimpse of who they are before we die? The stories in the following chapter provide us with some answers.

CHAPTER EIGHT

CROWDED ROOMS
AT THE END OF LIFE

"I believe we should adjourn this meeting to another place."
— final words of Adam Smith

The third type of deathbed experience I often hear about refers to "crowded rooms." As I've listened to these stories, I've been intrigued by the use of the words crowd *and* crowded. *When I started compiling examples to include in this book, I was surprised by how similar they were. In fact, it was hard to pick which ones to use because they were all so much alike. Now I realize that the very thing that makes them repetitious is also what makes them unique.*

Perhaps we don't have a full grasp of how many people we've touched in our lives. We don't remember everyone we've met, and we certainly can't recall all of the individuals who crossed our paths when we were children. In the tapestry of life and death, we may not always think about those who have come before us; we just know where we as individuals are positioned in the family tree. In dying, however, perhaps we're able to make the connections to the past that we'd missed earlier in life.

I often say that when someone is dying, it may be a "standing-room only" experience. And as I've stated previously, I firmly believe that just as loving hands greet us when we're born, loving arms will embrace us when we die.

Here's one of my own stories about a patient I had named Alice:

One afternoon I stopped by to visit Alice and her husband, Sal. The nurse told me that Sal had just left for the airport to pick up their son, who was flying in to be with his dying mother. As I entered the room, I found my patient, who was 79 years old, dozing. Not wanting to disturb her, I sat in the chair by her bed. When I got up to leave after a few minutes, I heard a soft voice ask, "Who are all these people?"

"It's only me, Alice," I said. "Were you having a dream?"

"No, I'm not dreaming. Just look at everyone."

"Who do you see?"

Instead of replying, she scooted up in the bed and asked me, "Why is it so crowded in here?"

I was perplexed when I first heard about the crowded-rooms perception from a dying patient, but I'd soon understand how common it was and perhaps what it meant. Over and over again, I'd hear dying patients talk about seeing a large group of people even when their rooms were empty. In some cases, those who had the crowded-room visions could tell me who each and every person was, but at other times they only recognized a few individuals.

I'd like to share another story from my first book, which is a good example of the crowded-room vision. A colleague once asked me to visit a patient of his who was a science professor. He'd said that Mr. Hill was dying and had a lot of questions that I might be able to help him with. Here's what happened:

As I approached Mr. Hill's hospital room, I wondered what kind of questions this 80-year-old would have. We chatted for a bit, and I learned that he'd been a widower for ten years and was retired. Then he got right to the point, requesting that I tell him how his body would "wind down."

I could see that the teacher in him wanted to understand all aspects of what he was going through, so I explained that dying is like shutting down a large factory filled with engines, assembly lines, and giant boilers. Everything doesn't suddenly go quiet when the "off" switch is pushed. Instead, the machinery creaks and moans as it slows to a halt.

We'd been talking for about 20 minutes when he looked away and glanced out his window.

"What is it?"

"I saw something last night that doesn't make sense. In the middle of the night, I woke up and my room was filled with people. I couldn't understand what was going on. I knew that doctors weren't making rounds with their students at that hour. I looked at the faces I saw—they went on and on. While I only knew some of them, they all seemed familiar. Then I had this realization that all of these individuals were dead. I even noticed a colleague from work who'd died five years ago from cancer."

We talked about the vision, and then I asked him to start naming the people in his life who had died.

"My wife."

"That's one."

"My parents and my in-laws."

"You also mentioned your colleague who had died as well as a student who had been killed in a car accident 20 years ago. That's seven people. Did you know your grandparents?"

"Yes, of course, but they died long ago."

"Where were they from?"

"Poland," Mr. Hill said. "My grandparents and their siblings—all nine of them—came to America within five years of each other. Some of them died before I was born, and they all died by the time I was ten." He paused to soak in the memories, and then he pointed out, "People passed away much younger in those days."

"That's true, but we're still talking about 18 or so people. That's certainly a large group, but let's not stop there. How many years did you teach?"

"I retired after 40 years."

He knew where I was going when I said, "I bet some of those students have died and you don't know about it. Most of their parents you'd interacted with are probably gone, too. I bet it *is* a crowded room."

He nodded and lay back contentedly on his pillow as if a complex question had finally been answered.

If we can accept that one person might greet us at the end of life, then couldn't <u>more than</u> one person be there? Let's go back to the other end of the spectrum: when a child is born, the waiting room in the maternity ward is usually overflowing with family and friends ready to welcome the newborn. Is it that much of a stretch, then, to assume that a crowd of well-wishers may be there to welcome us at death?

Crowded-room visions are nothing new to the dying and many of their caretakers. I'm excited to conclude this book with tales of this last type of deathbed phenomena.

◆

THE GOLDEN DOOR

by Teri

I'm a chaplain at a hospital, and I work with a wonderful administrative assistant named Martha, who's in her early 60s. One day she told me that her daughter, Dorothy, had a troubled life. She'd been a "difficult" child and had experienced a tumultuous adolescence.

Now as an adult, Dorothy was divorced and losing her battle with ovarian cancer. Because she was no longer able to work, she had to give up her apartment and move back in with her mother.

Martha welcomed her home and even painted the bedroom light blue, which was her daughter's favorite color. I'd visit them from time to time, and although Dorothy wasn't a regular churchgoer, she did believe in God.

Dorothy's condition worsened and her health rapidly deteriorated to the point that she was confined to her bed. Not long after, her mother noticed that she began looking up toward the corner of her room and would stare at a particular area on the wall.

One day when Dorothy was once again staring at the spot, she also blurted out, "Oh, it's a door. A lovely golden door."

Her mother thought that her comment was especially unusual because Dorothy seemed so nonchalant about it, as if a golden door appearing out of nowhere was commonplace. Curious, Martha asked, "Do you know why it's there?"

"I'm not sure . . . it isn't open yet."

"Do you know what's on the other side?"

"No, but I guess I'm going to find out soon," Dorothy replied.

Toward the end of her life, she'd mention the golden door more often, saying, "They're trying to push the door open."

"Who?" her mother asked.

"I don't know."

"You said 'they.' Do you think there's more than one person at the door?"

"Yes, I'm sure of it."

The following day, which was Dorothy's last, I was visiting and we were talking about God. In the middle of the conversation, she looked up toward the corner of the room and said, "They've pushed the door open!"

Martha had already told me about the golden door, so I asked, "Can I see them?"

"There they are!" Dorothy exclaimed. "Can't you see them? Oh, it's getting so crowded in here!"

Martha and I didn't know what to make of her comment. The only people in her room were the two of us and her nurse from hospice. That was hardly a crowd.

"Why do you say that it's so crowded?" I asked Dorothy.

"All of these people keep coming through the door, and it's getting packed in here."

Dorothy was slipping in and out of consciousness, but when she was awake, she'd point to the door and to everyone who was filling her room, saying, "Mom, look how many are here for me. They're going to help me." Hours before her death, she spoke only of the door and the crowd surrounding her. She was so happy. Moments before her death, her mother gently said, "Dorothy, you can go with these folks if it's time."

I placed my hand on the dying woman's and said, "It's all right to go. I'll take care of your mom."

Dorothy died very peacefully, and her mother was comforted by the fact that people were there for her. Although at first Martha didn't believe that the vision was real, as time went on she realized that the door and the crowd were exactly what her daughter needed.

I told Martha a few stories about other patients who had died seeing a crowd of people, and I assured her that the golden door was something heavenly.

EVERYONE IS THERE

by Kim

My work as a psychologist in a Catholic hospital is very fulfilling. I spend most of my time counseling teenagers in our well-being program.

My parents were always enormously proud of me. I was raised in a family of born-again Christians, and we attended church regularly. When my mom was stricken with a serious heart condition and had to prepare for surgery, our entire congregation was praying for her.

The operation went well, and my mother was out of the cardiac unit in record time, even starting to walk on her own again. Things were looking up and we were discussing the date of her discharge when she mentioned to a doctor that she felt like she was coming down with the flu.

A blood test showed a dramatic increase in my mom's white-blood-cell count, which indicated an infection. Her doctor immediately started her on antibiotics, but within 24 hours she was in the ICU, fighting a massive infection. My father and I couldn't have been more stunned when the doctor told us that we needed to make a decision about what to do if my mother's heart or lungs failed.

We prayed at Mom's bedside while members of our church gathered in the lobby to pray for a full recovery. At one point, I heard my mother mumbling, "Mommy, Daddy," as if she were a little girl. Not sure what was happening, I said, "It's okay, Mom. Everyone is praying, and God will help you recover."

"Mommy, Daddy," my mother repeated. "I'll come if I have to."

Alarmed and not sure who my mother was talking to, I said, "You have to stay here. God wants you to stay with us."

But my mother responded, "Everyone is there. There are so many people—I have to go."

Those were my mom's last words. I finally realized that she was seeing her deceased family, and there was nothing to be afraid of. Even though I was sad, I knew that death isn't something to fear.

When I prayed to God to keep my mother here, that was my will, not His. When God wants you, that's it, and my mom was ready to go to heaven.

Today I've taught my own children that even after I die, someday we'll all be together again. My mother's vision gave me a much deeper appreciation and faith in the promise of everlasting life. I also feel the gift of becoming a more compassionate and caring person. From what my mother saw in her last moments, I know firsthand that we live with God on a daily basis, because He sent my whole family to guide her to Him.

•◇•

THEY'RE ALL WAITING

by Jan

I'm a therapist who focuses more on education than having a private practice. I hold a Ph.D. in psychology and teach classes in a graduate program. I love my students' enthusiasm and get a kick out of hearing them say things like: "Oh, that's why I'm always mad at my boyfriend," or "Now I know why my mother and I don't get along—we're too much alike!"

I thought I'd heard it all until I listened to a story from Anil, one of my students from India. His father had died two years previously after a long illness, and he wanted to talk to me about Hindu views on death. This religion doesn't see death as an ending; rather, adherents believe that there are many more lifetimes to come. Anil was conflicted because he wasn't sure how his father's dying experience fit into his religious beliefs. This is what he told me:

> During the last two weeks of my father's life, he was still alert and at peace. The family knew that he was dying and made the funeral plans, which involved cremation because fire represents purification in Hinduism. We talked about karma, the belief that all deeds in the past would affect the present, and all decisions made now will impact the future.
>
> All of a sudden, my father became fixated on a point in the room. It was up in a corner, high above everyone's head. He suddenly said, "Mother is here." He was referring to his mother, and explained that she and his father were visiting him although my grandparents had died years ago. My dad kept staring at the same area on the wall and began naming

all the people who had stopped by to see him that day. Every day, more and more arrived—and every one of them had already died. Concerned, my mom pointed this fact out, but my father simply replied that it didn't matter.

Two days before my dad died, he said, "There are so many here—they're all waiting for me."

And moments before he left this world, Dad opened his eyes, smiled broadly, and told my mother, "Look. The lovely lady is here; Mother is here. She's calling, and it's time to go."

My father was smiling and staring at the same place until his face relaxed, his head sank back onto the pillow, and he stopped breathing and died.

My mom didn't know how to put his "crowded room" in the context of Hinduism. Shortly after his death, we went to see a Hindu priest who said all that mattered was that my father's experience brought him comfort. What more could you want from death?

Anil admitted that it took him a long time to tell his story to anyone. I told him that I admired his courage, and he thanked me for listening without passing judgment. I was amazed and humbled to hear such a powerful story.

· ◈ ·

MAYBE THEY WERE RIGHT

by Sonia

I love being a nurse at a large hospital. My unit caters to general medical issues and some postsurgical cases and cancer patients who need chemotherapy. I've seen my share of deathbed phenomena on the oncology unit during my 11 years there, but the story that I'll always carry with me is about my mother, Cara.

My mom was always very active. Even though she stopped driving in her 80s, she lived close to many of her favorite activities so that she could walk to them. She was a bingo fanatic and knew where every game in town was played. She also attended church regularly and enjoyed volunteering at the local nursing home.

When Mom was diagnosed with cancer, all of her family and friends took it hard. And for me, although I'd taken care of hundreds of patients who had cancer on my unit, now I had to picture my mother as a patient.

Life became filled with one round of chemotherapy after another. I thought that Mom should fight it at every step, but I also knew that it was an aggressive form of the disease. Tired of being nauseated all the time with no results, my mom decided to let nature take its course.

I convinced my mother to move in with me, and she was very independent at first. She cooked dinner for me and helped keep the house tidy, but soon became too weak for these tasks as her condition worsened. I switched to part-time work and eventually took a leave of absence to care for her.

As Mom's health deteriorated, I'd sometimes come into her room and find her looking up toward the corner and talking. Unfortunately, I knew this meant that she didn't have much time left.

"Who are you talking to?" I asked one day.

"Alvin. He's here, and he's waiting for me." Alvin was her husband, my father, who'd died nearly a decade ago.

"Dad is here?"

"Yes, of course!"

I found her attitude surprising. The mom I knew and loved would have never taken a conversation seriously that included talking to a dead person, but apparently that had all changed, as she began having regular chats with my dad.

One day I found my mother crying in her room. She was talking to my brother, who had tragically died in a car accident when he was a teenager. "It's just so wonderful to see him again," she told me later. "I never thought I would."

Other people came to visit as well. My mom was naming one dead relative after another, remarking, "Sonia, it's getting so crowded in here."

"That's what you get for entertaining so much," I teased.

The next day, my mother's tone shifted. "Well, they're here," she said with a degree of resignation. "They're calling me, but I'm not ready yet. I told them they have to wait because it's not time."

As Mom grew weaker and closer to death, she was in and out of a coma. When she was conscious, she told me, "I think it might be time. Maybe they were right."

Shortly before she died, she looked up toward that same corner of the wall and raised her hands as if she were reaching for something. Then she closed her eyes, and 15 minutes later, she died.

To this day, I wonder what my mother meant when she said, "Maybe they were right." Were they right that it was time for her to die? I'm just not sure, but I do believe that as we approach the end of life, we may see things that we don't fully understand.

As a nurse, I'm well aware that visions are often attributed to oxygen deprivation or some sort of physiological aberration. However, many of my patients have these experiences weeks before death when a lack of oxygen can't be blamed. These incidents happen so often that they can no longer be dismissed.

AN INVITATION

by Lainey

About ten years ago, I started working in end-of-life care as a social worker. Those of us in this field get sort of desensitized to death because for us, it's an everyday event. And although people often think that my job must be depressing, they don't understand the gifts that come out of it.

I currently spend a good bit of time in a general hospice inpatient unit, where we function as the go-to people to counsel dying individuals and their families.

The hospice employees seek my team and me out if they want to share something or check out whether or not a situation is normal. We become the staff shrinks in a sense. New team members also come to us when a dead loved one appears to a patient. They ask questions like: "What should I do? Have you seen anything like this before? They aren't on opiates, but they keep having visions—what is it? Could it be real? What if I think it's real? Am *I* crazy?" We've seen and heard it all. In fact, there isn't a hospice team anywhere that doesn't have these kinds of stories. I think they're fascinating because they're so similar and yet unique to each individual. One patient especially stands out in my mind.

Mrs. Riley was 78 years old, and she was "unrepresented," meaning that she had no family. As her health declined, the nursing home got a conservator for her. Luckily, she'd put her wishes in writing so it was clear what she wanted at the end of her life.

Mrs. Riley was assigned to one of our newer hospice nurses, Katie, who was in her 20s and had previously worked in the oncology unit of the hospital. Katie loved helping people and hoped to have more contact with patients in hospice.

I wasn't surprised when Katie appeared at my office door, requesting that I visit Mrs. Riley with her. I knew something was up, so I agreed to go but asked her to update me first. After filling me in on all of Mrs. Riley's medical history, she hesitantly told me, "I heard her call out 'Mommy.' I think she thinks that I'm her mother, but when she repeated it, she was looking over and past me, as if I weren't there."

"Do you think she might be having a vision of her dead mother?"

"Do we know for sure that her mother is dead?" Katie inquired.

"No, we don't, but if she was alive, don't you think she'd come in the front door rather than appear over your head?"

Katie didn't find my sarcasm amusing, but I went on. "Seriously, Katie, why not just accept it for what it is? The patient believes her mother is there, and what could be more comforting than having your mom with you at the end of your life? Why not treat it as reality? You can't argue with her and say that she isn't there. There's no point in that."

"Thanks, Lainey. You've given me a lot to think about. I guess I can try to accept that her mom is coming to visit."

The next day, however, the young nurse pulled me aside in the hallway, and in a worried voice, said, "Okay, I was getting used to Mrs. Riley's mom being there, but now Dad has shown up, too."

I tried to explain how common and comforting this is to the patient. "Don't you think it would be arrogant to tell someone that what they're seeing isn't real?" I asked Katie. "How can you know for sure? How do you prove that someone isn't seeing a deceased loved one? While you're at it, try proving whether or not the afterlife exists, too. As far as Mrs. Riley goes, she has her parents with her; and she also has you, a caring, compassionate nurse."

I meant every word of it. Katie *was* a good nurse who truly cared for all of her patients—she just knew more about pain and symptom management than she did about deathbed phenomena. The next day, like clockwork, Katie called and asked me to meet her in Mrs. Riley's room. As I headed down the familiar hallway, all I could think was, *Doesn't she ever take a day off?*

When I got to her room, Mrs. Riley didn't look like she was in pain, but she seemed to be mumbling something.

"Listen to what she's saying," Katie said, so I pulled up a chair, sat down, and leaned in.

"There are so many of you," Mrs. Riley softly remarked.

"So many of who?" I asked.

"I don't know." Then she clearly said, "You are all so young—still so young."

"Do you know why they're here, Mrs. Riley?" I asked.

"They're inviting me to join them."

"How many are there?"

"So many," she replied. "It's so crowded. I can't believe that so many are here."

"Do you recognize anyone?"

"I can't really see their faces—only some. It's blurry. I do see Timothy, though. He was my first."

"First what?"

"My first student to die."

Katie grabbed my arm tightly as I continued asking Mrs. Riley questions. "It's so nice that your parents and your students wanted to see you. You must have been a wonderful teacher."

"Nice," was all she said.

When the young nurse and I left the room, she started treating me like I was some sort of spirit communicator. She peppered me with questions, such as, "How did you do that?

How did you know she was a teacher, too? Did you guess, or did you know intuitively?"

I would have loved to take credit for being psychic and all powerful, but I decided to tell Katie the truth. "I read her history on file and found out she taught for more than 40 years. I thought that maybe teachers are comforted by their former students in their hallucinations. Or maybe certain students were coming to her because she played a significant role in their lives. Regardless, Mrs. Riley seems content and comfortable, and that's all that matters. I know it's unusual, but in time, you'll get used to your patients' visions."

At the end of the day, the staff had a long discussion about Mrs. Riley. She'd been single her whole life and was totally devoted to teaching. We debated if her vision of all those children whom she couldn't clearly see represented the students she'd taught during four decades. She had no family, yet she was never frightened by the experience. She died peacefully . . . and, unbeknownst to her, she taught Katie a lot about the end of life.

DON'T TALK TO THE CROWD

by Rita

I'm a social worker at a rural hospital. One patient I'll never forget was a 75-year-old woman who had been diagnosed with colon cancer. Annie was a realist and very grounded—she said that she'd lived a productive life and was ready to hear the truth about her diagnosis and accept it. However, her family (particularly her daughter, April) kept insisting that there was nothing that she couldn't overcome. They loved her and wanted her to stick around so much that they kept convincing themselves that their mother was getting better, but in truth, she wasn't.

Before Annie's health started to decline, she used to have a great deal of energy. Now she slept more and spoke less. In the space of a few weeks, in fact, she stopped talking altogether and spent most of her time dozing. Her loved ones felt helpless and sat in silence with her, making sure that she wasn't in pain. But one afternoon, she woke up, sat up in bed, and began to speak quite clearly.

The family felt instantly hopeful. Maybe she was coming out of her illness, they told each other.

I hated to be the one to rain on their parade, but I told my patient's loved ones that her sudden clarity of speech wasn't a sign that she was on the mend; rather, it meant that she was experiencing one last rally before death.

As if my bad news wasn't enough, although Annie was able to speak again, she wasn't communicating with her family. Instead, she was talking to invisible people in the corner of her room.

"Mom, who are you talking to?" April asked.

"Why, people I've known my whole my life. They've

been gone a long time, but they're here to see me. So many of them—what a crowd!"

"Don't talk to them. Stay with us."

April was alarmed and came to find me at the nurse's station. "I think there's something wrong with my mother," she said. "She keeps speaking to people she thinks she's seeing. I think she's hallucinating because she told me that there's a large number of her deceased family members visiting her in the room."

Before I had a chance to respond, a nurse who was working behind the desk and had overheard us talking said, "Don't worry. It's a good sign that your mother can see a group of people waiting to welcome her. She obviously doesn't feel alone or scared. This is a common occurrence right before someone dies."

I told April that as a social worker, I see this all the time, too. I hoped this information would help her understand that her mom wasn't going crazy or hallucinating.

This is how we as caregivers attempt to calm the waters. In addition to comforting our patients, we often spend a lot of time reassuring and consoling family members when their loved ones are close to death.

After our talk, April seemed more relaxed and okay with her mother's visions. I think it became sort of a tipping point for her so that she'd finally acknowledge that her mom wasn't going to get better. In the end, Annie died at home, content and at peace. For this, her family was very grateful.

I have to say that deathbed visions—especially those of crowds surrounding the dying person—occur more often than most of us realize, and I genuinely believe they're real. Most people's initial reaction is disbelief or fear, but when we talk about it, it can be very comforting to know that our loved ones are taken care of as they leave this world for the next.

· ◇ ·

My journey of writing this book is coming to an end, but my exploration will continue—and I hope that this will be the beginning of yours.

My wish is that you'll share these stories and start a conversation. Talk to others and ask about their stories. I believe that each and every one of us can find someone who has experienced the deathbed vision of a loved one. You never know: who and what you see before you die might be as close as a family member, friend, co-worker, or neighbor.

In life, we're more connected to others than we ever imagined. What if we're even more connected in death? Perhaps heaven is closer than we think.

EPILOGUE

A recent pilot study examined the incidence of death-bed visions and their effects on the dying as well as on those who work in the health-care industry. Conducted by the palliative-care team at Camden Primary Care Trust in London, their findings were as follows:

> Interviews revealed that patients regularly report these phenomena as an important part of their dying process, and that DBP [deathbed phenomena] are far broader than the traditional image of an apparition at the end of the bed. Results of the interviews raise concerns about the lack of education or training to help palliative-care teams recognize the wider implications of DBP and deal with difficult questions or situations associated with them. Many DBP may go unreported because of this. Results of this pilot study also suggest that DBP aren't drug-induced, and that patients would rather talk to nurses than doctors about their dying experiences.

My belief is that many health-care workers haven't been trained to view death as an important part of life. I had the privilege of spending time with Mother Teresa, and she once told me that "death is part of the achievement of life." Our traditional Western medical system is far from perceiving death as the "achievement of life," however. In fact, mainstream medicine still considers it a "failure." Death remains an enemy and is the result of a battle that was lost.

If physicians see death as the result of their own inability to save every life all the time, how would they view a phenomenon that usually occurs on their day of defeat? When I began to write my first book in 1995, I spoke to an oncologist about being around the dying, specifically watching a person die. To my amazement, he replied that he hadn't spent much time with patients who were very close to death. "But some of your patients die, right?" I asked.

"Yes, 30 to 40 percent."

"Then how do you not see it?"

"They don't need much from me at that point for symptom management," he said. "Their primary physician focuses on them, and I move on to other patients."

I pressed him further. "Have you ever been in the room when a patient died?"

"No."

Many assume that to be in medicine means you've seen death firsthand, but clearly, this oncologist represents those in the field who are inexperienced and uncomfortable with it.

There was much this individual needed to learn. For his patients, after waging a two- to five-year battle with cancer and seeing their doctor weekly or monthly, this was a relationship that transcended just "symptom management." Physicians like him need to learn that there's value for the patients—and even for them—in continuing contact up to the end. This personal anecdote helped me understand why a lot of health-care workers may not be open to (much less act as great historians of) deathbed visions, and why patients may not feel comfortable to share such events with them.

As many of the stories in the book have illustrated, those who are at the end of their lives are often reluctant to talk about deathbed phenomena, due to fear of ridicule, dismissal, or even being labeled as "crazy." Although I also think these stories prove that just because someone is dying and may be peering into the next world, it doesn't mean that he or she is no longer aware of and connected to this world.

Family members and friends also attempt to manage their feelings about loved ones experiencing visions in an environment that often doesn't recognize or validate them. They may feel ashamed, not realizing how common these extraordinary episodes are. Moreover, in our loved ones' last days, most of us focus on ensuring that their care is good and that they aren't suffering. We're also overwhelmed at times by our own grief, searching for hope even when there is none. So it's difficult to imagine that in the midst of all this, a relative or friend would want to go through the possible embarrassment and questioning of a near-death awareness. Perhaps if they knew that in the legal world a person's final words are more highly valued and examined, they might view these visions differently or at least be more at peace.

In the study I cited earlier, many health-care workers interviewed stated that deathbed visions could be viewed as a prognostic indicator for nearing death, and that they "were in agreement that helping patients to become reconciled with their life is an important part of palliative care work."

There can be no end to this book because the human story is ongoing. There are so many more stories to be told. I hope that health-care professionals and family members who haven't come forth about the deathbed visions they've experienced might be a little more comfortable to finally talk about them, knowing that they aren't alone.

Likewise, additional studies on deathbed visions need to be conducted despite the fact that there are no lucrative products or treatments that would result from gaining more insights into the phenomenon. Just because a question may not have an answer—just because it's a mystery that we may never totally solve—that doesn't mean we shouldn't bring it to the forefront.

Unlike people who have near-death experiences (NDE) and live to tell their stories, write about them, and bring them into our cultural discussion, the deathbed-vision witness has obviously died. NDE survivors may feel a sense of awe and even be proud of the fact that they survived death and lived to talk about it. For the grieving who have just lost loved ones, though, there isn't the same incentive to share their stories about a vision that the dying person experienced.

We must reevaluate our reaction to events beyond our understanding. Doesn't this matter deserve our attention and open-mindedness now more than ever? As we strive to improve the care of the dying, are we missing something by not including deathbed visions in the quest for a peaceful and meaningful death?

Today we often assume that the only thing available to comfort the dying is more technology or better symptom management. I believe that God and nature have already built in a means of comfort by providing us with visions, and who and what we see before we die is just as vital as the cutting-edge medical breakthroughs that will continue to advance the health-care industry.

While death may look like a loss to the living, the last hours of a dying person may very well be filled with fullness rather than emptiness. No matter how death unfolds for us—whether we're planning for a "trip," or gazing upon our loved ones or a crowded bedroom in awe—our transition ultimately is a mystery. Sometimes all we can do is embrace the unknown and unexplainable.

The saying goes, "We come into this world alone, and we leave alone." We've been brought up to believe that dying is a lonely, solitary event. But what if everything we know isn't true?

What if the long road that you thought you'll eventually have to walk alone has unseen companions? What if who and what you see before you die changes everything?

◆

AFTERTHOUGHTS

Author's note: May 2011: During the past year, I've received a tremendous response to this book. Readers have sent me their comments, questions, and even more stories about deathbed visions. Here's what I experienced after the publication of the book, as well as some insights I gleaned on my own exploration of the afterlife. I hope the conversation never ends. . . .

Books are usually a one-way conversation in that the author shares information with his or her readers. Other than checking out a published review or chatting with those who attend a book signing or lecture, the writer doesn't tend to get a lot of feedback. However, the Internet has drastically changed all that. Today, I can write a book such as this one, or post an article online, and draw almost immediate responses to the work.

Since the publication of *Visions, Trips, and Crowded Rooms* in 2010, I've received countless e-mails and thousands of comments about it, as well as responses to the articles I've written on the topic. It amazes me that I could end up with more than 1,000 pages of comments for a book that was only 160 pages. Now, a year after the hardcover has come out, I've decided to rejoin the conversation and share my thoughts on the responses and questions I received during this time.

I would be dishonest if I didn't acknowledge my anxiety about giving deathbed visions center stage in my writing. When I initially brought up the subject in my first book, *The Needs of the Dying,* I told an editor I knew that I might want to do an entire book on it someday. The response I received was: "It could ruin your credibility! Do you think a lot of people believe that this really happens?" I timidly replied that it *does* happen, whether I presented the information or not.

I understood where this person was coming from. I expressed the same fear when my mentor, Elisabeth Kübler-Ross, mentioned a similar notion to me years ago. I thought, *I'm not going there. People will think I'm nuts!* But then after a couple of decades, and with a lot more courage and respect for the truth, I did decide to "go public." The notion of deathbed visions, I surmised, was kind of like gravity—existing regardless of what I (or others) say about the subject. Similarly, deathbed visions occur whether or not we choose to believe in them. My job for my new book was to simply report my findings, and the overwhelming conclusion was that not only are they *real*, but they're also quite *common*.

The majority of the responses I received can be summed up in one story. A CNN producer loved my book and wanted to interview me, but she wasn't sure how a room full of reporters and other colleagues would accept the premise of the dead greeting the dying. After the producer presented the idea for a story, she waited to see if her associates would think it was worth looking into or shrug it off as just plain nonsense. What happened next was the last thing she'd expected. All of a sudden, these tough, fact-driven men and women started sharing stories about their own loved ones who had experienced deathbed visions shortly before they died. As the producer later told me, "I realized that what you said was true. So many people have witnessed this or know someone who has but never told anyone about it." And once again, a room full of people who had never discussed such a subject related stories that were strikingly similar. The positive response this producer received led to an appearance on CNN.

Not long after my book was published, I became a contributing writer for **Oprah.com** on topics relating to grief and loss. A friend said, "Oprah has a high bar—make sure your work is always up to her standards!" I know high bars. When your first book gets praised by Mother Teresa, you understand the importance of people putting their trust in you and your work. With that in mind, I wrote an article highlighting the main points of my book, called "What We Can't Explain at the End of Life: Who and What You See Before You Die." Between Facebook "likes" and user comments, the response was huge. And when that many people decide to post something, I can only imagine how many others just read the article. All of the comments were very thoughtful and validating of the phenomenon, and it was thrilling to reach such a large audience.

Interestingly, the Internet wasn't the only place in the past year that "visited" the afterlife and sparked an intense debate—there was also the movie *Hereafter,* which was directed by Clint Eastwood and starred Matt Damon. When the movie was released, I was asked to do some press for it. One of the first things people noticed was that the artwork for the film's poster and promotion—a blurred image of a crowd of people greeting the dying—was surprisingly similar to the cover of my own book. It's yet another example of this recurring theme: even the ways in which artists interpret the afterlife have commonalities. In the movie, my "counterpart" meets with one of the lead characters and says that the accounts of what the dying experience are so strikingly similar that they couldn't merely be coincidental. Those are the very same words that roll off my tongue all too often and reflect the contents of this book. It was fascinating to actually hear the words on the big screen that *I* have so often used to describe the experience of the dying.

The CNN appearance began to air just around that time, and on the TV segment we also discussed an article I wrote for CNN's website. The avalanche of responses and even more personal stories I received to both was astounding. For the sake of reading, they would be terribly repetitious to include here. But if you were to see the thousands of responses, you'd have to ask yourself how so many people all over the world who are dying could have the same experiences. That is also what makes this phenomenon so amazing. There were stories, accounts from health-care professionals, and even videos by family members describing what they'd witnessed.

The article on **CNN.com** also served as a forum for those who don't believe in deathbed visions to voice their opinions. I first noticed that many of the critical responses mirrored what someone asked me after reading my book: "Why did you just choose the stories that described dying people having the same experiences?" My response was that I didn't handpick certain stories—that is just what the dying reported!

Denying the reality of the dying doesn't make sense. One person wrote that although he hadn't been around someone who was close to death, one thing was clear to him: When we die, that's it. There are no reunions, no heaven or hell, no new consciousness, no loved ones greeting us . . . *nothing.* He believed that to think anything else was ignorant and arrogant.

My compassionate response to this person is that someday he'll lose a loved one, and he might actually witness the phenomenon for himself. In the meantime, why deny someone else's reality? We can only deny or validate our own experiences when it comes to observing the dying. How can one of us tell another that his or her experience isn't real?

A lot of skeptics also brought up the fact that deathbed visions and other occurrences could be explained by severe conditions such as dementia or the effects of a human body as it starts to shut down. There is no doubt that diseases such as Alzheimer's and cancer—as well as the presence of opiates to control pain, the limited ability to take in oxygen, and the release of chemicals in the brain (and a million other factors)—can affect the way in which people die. The reality is that the only ones who know for certain are already on the other side. Only the dead know the truth—the rest of us just witness the phenomenon. Even if deathbed visions could solely be attributed to the actions of a dying brain, there wouldn't be such a shocking shared pattern of memory release or "hallucinations" that are practically identical. That would be like saying that tissue death happens in a specific pattern in everyone, all the time.

We do live and die differently. Every life has its own unique belief systems, culture, and language. We even die at different speeds. Yet when we see the dying, and hear from their loved ones, the end results are amazingly similar. How is that possible?

We can't fully explain how the Egyptians built the pyramids. Perhaps it was done by slaves over more years than we can comprehend, or maybe it was aliens. We don't know for sure, but we don't debate whether the pyramids exist; rather, we focus on the how and why. Of course what makes the argument more tangible is that the pyramids are physically present. We can see and touch them, so we don't doubt their existence. Yet to anyone who has been in the room when the dead greet the dying, this is just as real. Unfortunately, we haven't yet moved to the "let's find out why" discussion. We are stuck between those who have witnessed the phenomenon and those who haven't.

Deaths and births are like snowflakes—each one is unique *and* very similar. We die in a million ways, in a million places, with billions of variables. Yet the visions of the dying are so often unbelievably similar. Why is this so? Some have raised the theory that it is the brain's way of psychologically making it easier to die; that is, our brains are comforting and protecting us. If this is the case, though, why don't we see a vision of our favorite places, our kids, or our other living loved ones? Why don't the dying ever report a vision of a doctor, nurse, or a cherished stuffed animal? Why don't we see Puff the Magic Dragon or our favorite armchair?

Recently, I was visiting a dying woman who loved watching Katie Couric on the evening news. She never missed a broadcast. When the woman and I were chatting, she told me that while growing up, she'd watch Walter Cronkite every night with her mother and stepfather. Her never-to-be-realized dream was that someday she would meet Walter Cronkite or Katie Couric. She later shared that her birth father died when she was four years old . . . and he was now visiting her on her deathbed. So if deathbed visions are a trick of the mind, then why did this woman's father, whom she barely knew, visit her? Why didn't Katie Couric or Walter Cronkite come to call?

This is the question we can't answer, but if you spend enough time among the dying, that question is ever present. Spend some time with the dying and you'll learn a lot of humility and respect for the mystery of the dying process. Anyone who walks into a hospice thinking that they know it all will eventually learn that having all of the answers is just not possible.

Some of the comments I received insisted that those who experience or believe in deathbed visions are just letting their faith and hopes get out of control—they are so desperate for an afterlife that they invent it. Well, most of us have faith in something. Those who say that there is nothing when we die have faith, too. They just have faith that there is nothing. I'm not sure who told them that or where they got their information, but I do know that the dying don't say, "Here comes nothing. I now see nothing." And health-care professionals don't report that the dying speak of entering a "nothingness." I'm going to believe the words of the dying over the beliefs and doubts of the living who haven't lost a loved one or worked in a hospital or hospice setting.

So the conversation continues. I strongly believe that we should keep exploring, keep sharing. My hope for *Visions, Trips, and Crowded Rooms* was to send the same message that Elisabeth Kübler-Ross espoused decades earlier: *We need to listen to the dying. If we allow the dying to be our teachers, we will have open hearts and minds.*

We can finally come to terms with our fear of death, understanding that perhaps it's not an ending but a continuation. We don't know what's on the other side, but the dying are clearly telling us that there *is* another side. Now it's up to us. Will we listen?

Family members are so grateful when they learn that deathbed visions are a common, normal occurrence. Knowing that their loved one was not "going crazy" or "talking nonsense" can be a tremendous relief and comfort. I hope that everyone keeps the dialogue going, commenting online and sharing their experiences.

I'd love it if *you* would share your stories, reports, and videos with me. You can always find me at: **David@grief .com**. And visit **www.grief.com** to see some of the videos and read the articles discussed in this section. Remember, the more we share, the more we may truly realize that love never dies.

ACKNOWLEDGMENTS

First and foremost, I want to thank all of the wonderful people who were willing to share their stories with me. I would thank each of you here if it weren't for the fact that most people, especially health-care professionals, request anonymity when discussing deathbed visions. Let's hope that your contribution will help others feel less alone in their experiences.

My professional thanks go to Jennifer Rudolph Walsh and Erin Malone, my agents at William Morris Endeavor Entertainment. Jennifer, thank you for being there when I win awards, but more important, thanks for being by my side when I don't. Erin, I'm grateful to you for making this book a reality. Thank you for ensuring that my manuscripts are ones that publishers will want to turn into books. I love you for always wanting my writing to be the best it can be.

Reid Tracy, thank you for welcoming me into Hay House and giving this book a home. Thanks to Jill Kramer for overseeing the editing process; and to Lisa Mitchell, for doing such an extraordinary job editing the work. And, of course, thank you, Louise Hay. Who could have imagined that when we worked together almost 25 years ago, we would be connected again in an incredible publishing house that you created?

Andrea Cagan, as always you keep my hands on the keyboard and help me focus when the world pulls me in a million different directions. Linda Hewitt, my dear friend, we've been together for so many years I've lost count. No matter what I'm doing or where I am, you're always there for me. I appreciate you more than you know.

My gratitude goes to Nick Owchar, the deputy book editor for the *Los Angeles Times*. Nick, my chapter on the arts wouldn't have been possible without you. Thank you for inviting me into the world of book reviews and enabling me to have a voice in the book reviewer's world as well as at the *L.A. Times*. Thank you for your fine writing here and there.

To my friends: Ann Massie, thanks for your support as well as your porch to finish writing this book on. To Carmen Carrillo, thank you for always being a great nurse and person. For Annie Gad and Adele Bass, you've both been a true gift to me.

And to my colleagues at Citrus Valley Health Partners and Citrus Valley Hospice: thank you, Robert Curry and Elvia Foulke for the opportunity to work in an environment that encourages and challenges me every day and reminds me what's important. Thanks also to Lori Oberon and Sandy Plouffe.

And to the two women who got me here: Elisabeth Kübler-Ross in heaven and Marianne Williamson on Earth, my thanks are beyond words. You both mean the world to me.

To my goddaughter, India, who is more than I could have ever hoped for in this lifetime. You've brought such joy and hope to my world in ways I've never dreamed possible. I love you so much.

And to my sons, Richard and David, thank you for helping me understand how deep love can go. I'm infinitely grateful for the richness you've brought into my life.

I promise you, Richard, David, and India . . . if there is a way, I will be there.

About the Author

David Kessler is one of the most well-known experts and lecturers on death and dying and grief and loss. He co-authored two bestsellers with the legendary Elisabeth Kübler-Ross: *On Grief and Grieving* and *Life Lessons*. Kessler was honored to have been with Kübler-Ross during her passing.

His first book, *The Needs of the Dying*, a #1 best-selling hospice book, received praise by Mother Teresa. His services have been used by Elizabeth Taylor, Jamie Lee Curtis, and Marianne Williamson when their loved ones faced life-challenging illnesses. He also worked with late actors Anthony Perkins and Michael Landon.

Kessler has appeared on CNN, NBC, PBS, and *Entertainment Tonight*. He has been interviewed on *Oprah & Friends*, and his work has been featured in *The New York Times*, *The New Yorker*, and *People* magazine. He has written for *The Boston Globe*, the *San Francisco Chronicle*, *The Wall Street Journal*, and *Anderson Cooper 360°*; and he now writes book reviews for the *Los Angeles Times*. He is also a contributing writer for **Oprah.com** as well as an **AOL.com** Health Expert. Kessler has been a guest on national television shows to discuss Michael Jackson's death, and he was mentioned in the book *My Journey with Farrah*, about Alana Stewart and Farrah Fawcett. For more information, please visit **www.Grief.com**.

We hope you enjoyed this Hay House book. If you'd like to receive our online catalog featuring additional information on Hay House books and products, or if you'd like to find out more about the Hay Foundation, please contact:

Hay House, Inc., P.O. Box 5100, Carlsbad, CA 92018-5100
(760) 431-7695 or (800) 654-5126
(760) 431-6948 (fax) or (800) 650-5115 (fax)
www.hayhouse.com® • www.hayfoundation.org

———

Published in Australia by: Hay House Australia Pty. Ltd.,
18/36 Ralph St., Alexandria NSW 2015
Phone: 612-9669-4299 • *Fax:* 612-9669-4144
www.hayhouse.com.au

Published in the United Kingdom by: Hay House UK, Ltd.,
The Sixth Floor, Watson House, 54 Baker Street, London W1U 7BU
Phone: +44 (0)20 3927 7290 • *Fax:* +44 (0)20 3927 7291
www.hayhouse.co.uk

Published in India by: Hay House Publishers India,
Muskaan Complex, Plot No. 3, B-2, Vasant Kunj, New Delhi 110 070
Phone: 91-11-4176-1620 • *Fax:* 91-11-4176-1630
www.hayhouse.co.in

———

Access New Knowledge.
Anytime. Anywhere.

Learn and evolve at your own pace
with the world's leading experts.

www.hayhouseU.com